Meet the Kinect

An Introduction to Programming Natural User
Interfaces

Sean Kean
Jonathan C. Hall
Phoenix Perry

Apress®

Meet the Kinect: An Introduction to Programming Natural User Interfaces

ISBN-13 (pbk): 978-1-4302-3888-1

ISBN-13 (electronic): 978-1-4302-3889-8

President and Publisher: Paul Manning
Lead Editor: Jonathan Gennick
Technical Reviewer: Jarrett Webb
Editorial Board: Steve Anglin, Mark Beckner, Ewan Buckingham, Gary Cornell, Morgan Ertel, Jonathan Gennick, Jonathan Hassell, Robert Hutchinson, Michelle Lowman, James Markham, Matthew Moodie, Jeff Olson, Jeffrey Pepper, Douglas Pundick, Ben Renow-Clarke, Dominic Shakeshaft, Gwenan Spearing, Matt Wade, Tom Welsh
Coordinating Editor: Anita Castro
Copy Editor: Scribendi.com
Compositor: Bytheway Publishing Services
Indexer: SPI Global
Artist: SPI Global
Cover Designer: Anna Ishchenko

Distributed to the book trade worldwide by Springer Science+Business Media New York, 233 Spring Street, 6th Floor, New York, NY 10013. Phone 1-800-SPRINGER, fax (201) 348-4505, e-mail orders-ny@springer-sbm.com, or visit www.springeronline.com.

For information regarding translations, please e-mail rights@apress.com, or visit www.apress.com.

Apress and friends of ED books may be purchased in bulk for academic, corporate, or promotional use. eBook versions and licenses are also available for most titles. For more information, reference our Special Bulk Sales–eBook Licensing web page at www.apress.com/bulk-sales.

Any source code or other supplementary materials referenced by the author in this text are available to readers at www.apress.com. For detailed information about how to locate your book's source code, go to www.apress.com/source-code/.

Dedicated to Christa Erickson: artist, educator, flaneuse, and esteemed mentor.

—Sean Kean

Contents at a Glance

Contents

About the Authors

 **Sean Kean** is an artist and entrepreneur living in Brooklyn, New York. With a background spanning engineering, art, education, and travel, he is passionate about simplifying complex technology in order to make tools more accessible to others. Insatiable in his curiosity, the author has filled his passport as a flight attendant, rediscovered learning through play as an early childhood educator, studied the streets and buildings of New York City in order to earn both a taxi driver license and real estate sales license, and has been programming well enough to be dangerous for more than 20 years. Sean is currently working to bridge the gap between the physical and digital worlds at HERE, Inc. (http://here.st), to bring volumetric 3D TVs mainstream with the VoxieBox (www.voxiebox.com), and to help professionals working with volumetric depth cameras, software, and displays to connect to each other through the Volumetric Society (www.volumetric.org) via a publication, conference, and local chapter meetups you can help set up in your city.

 **Jonathan C. Hall** is one of the creators of Sensecast, an application that makes it easy to build motion-controlled interfaces for content using a Kinect. He has been an independent designer/developer for digital projects for the last decade. Hall has also done stints as a beat reporter, a researcher for the smartest person in the world, a technology consultant to the likes of Rob Jarvik and King Abdullah II of Jordan, and a student of the sciences and humanities. Jonathan holds a BA from Harvard University, where he studied languages and religion, and about half a PhD (Communications) from Columbia University.

 **Phoenix Perry** was born in Denver, CO, in 1975. From digital arts curator to Creative Director, she has gained extensive experience in new media, design, and user interfaces. Perry's work spans a large range of disciplines, including drawing, generative art, video, games, and sound. Her projects have been seen worldwide at venues and festivals, including Come out and Play, the Maker Faire at the New York Hall of Science, the Lincoln Center, Transmediale, the Yerba Buena Center for the Arts, the LAMCA, Harvest Works, Babycastles, the European Media Arts Festival, GenArt, the Seoul Film Festival, and Harvestworks. She is adjunct faculty at NYU-Poly in Integrated Digital Media and owns Devotion Gallery in Brooklyn, NY.

About the Technical Reviewer

Jarrett Webb creates imaginative, dynamic, interactive, immersive experiences using multi-touch technology and the Kinect. He lives in Austin, TX.

Acknowledgments

With deep gratitude to my parents and to my wife, Kate, who have supported even my most ill-advised endeavors.

Jonathan C. Hall

My thanks to Amir Hirsch, Alona Lerman, the OpenKinect community, and the amazing team at Apress for helping make this book possible.

Phoenix Perry

CHAPTER 1

Getting Started

In this chapter you'll unbox a new Kinect—or if you have one already, you'll disconnect it from your Xbox. Then you'll install some software, plug the Kinect into a computer, and take a look at what all of the fuss is about with this unique device. You'll learn what the different components of the Kinect are and be able to play with some simple controls to get a feel for how all the parts work together to make the magic happen.

The Kinect is marketed, packaged, and designed for use with Microsoft's Xbox gaming console. The Xbox is a remarkable living room entertainment system, and if you haven't tried Dance Central or Kinect Sports, I recommend that you do—playing those two games at the 24-hour Best Buy in Union Square here in NYC is what got me so excited about the Kinect in the first place. I dragged as many friends as I could down to the store so they could see this amazing technology in action.

That said, this book is the unofficial manual for how to take a Kinect and use it outside the living room—no Xbox required. Now, let's make sure you have everything you need to unplug your Kinect from the game system—or purchase one by itself, plug it into your computer, and get tinkering.

Buying the Correct Kinect

When I wanted to get my own Kinect, I spent a lot of time trying to figure out the right product to buy out of all of the Xbox Kinect–branded merchandise. I really wanted to play the Xbox games *and* have a Kinect that could work on my computer. Unfortunately, the Xbox Kinect system bundle isn't packaged with this goal in mind.

I ended up deciding to purchase the standalone Kinect sensor (Figure 1-1) and saved some money by getting a used Xbox system on which to play the games. The standalone Kinect sensor package includes an adapter cable that lets your Kinect draw power directly from a wall outlet instead of from the Xbox console.

Figure 1-1. *Kinect Sensor with Kinect Adventures!—The* **only** *Xbox Kinect product that comes with all the parts ready to hook up to your computer.*

Another option is to buy the Kinect bundle that includes an Xbox console and the Kinect sensor. You see that bundle as the second item in Figure 1-2. The danger is that people often purchase the Kinect bundle thinking that it will immediately work for them…until they bring it home and find that they are missing a cable and now have to buy one online and wait for it to arrive.

What the Kinect bundle lacks is the power adapter that you need in order to use your Kinect with a personal computer via USB. While I fully endorse getting the full Xbox Kinect system bundle, you'll need to purchase this additional accessory, a US $30 power adapter, to be able to connect the Kinect to your computer via normal USB. Figure 1-2 shows that power adapter, which is the third item listed in the figure.

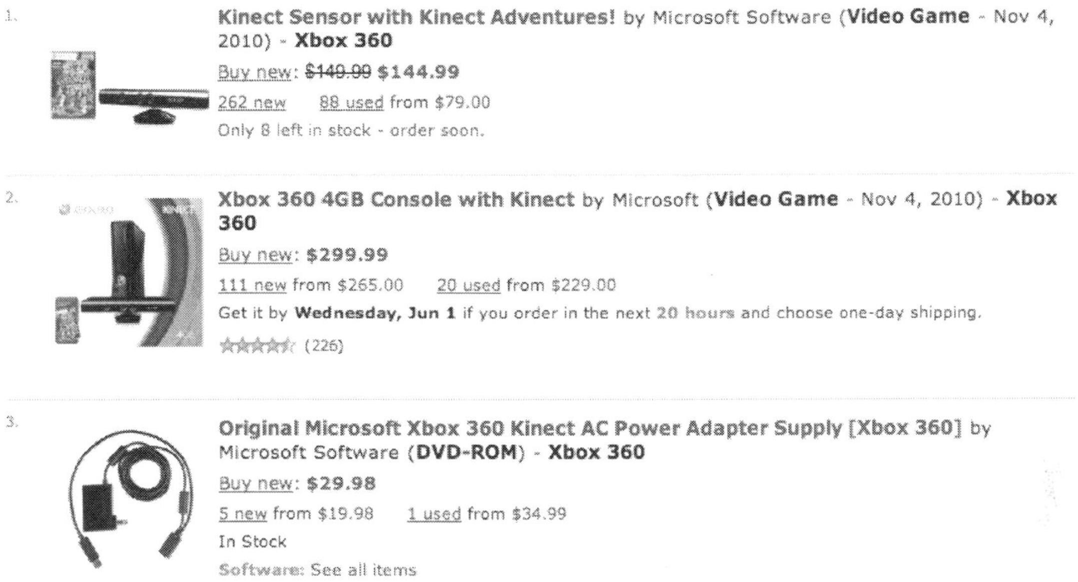

1. **Kinect Sensor with Kinect Adventures!** by Microsoft Software (**Video Game** - Nov 4, 2010) - **Xbox 360**

   Buy new: $~~$149.99~~ $144.99

   262 new   88 used from $79.00

   Only 8 left in stock - order soon.

2. **Xbox 360 4GB Console with Kinect** by Microsoft (**Video Game** - Nov 4, 2010) - **Xbox 360**

   Buy new: $299.99

   111 new from $265.00   20 used from $229.00

   Get it by **Wednesday, Jun 1** if you order in the next 20 hours and choose one-day shipping.

   ★★★★☆ (226)

3. **Original Microsoft Xbox 360 Kinect AC Power Adapter Supply [Xbox 360]** by Microsoft Software (**DVD-ROM**) - **Xbox 360**

   Buy new: $29.98

   5 new from $19.98   1 used from $34.99

   In Stock

   Software: See all items

Figure 1-2. Online product listings on Amazon.com for Kinect-related products—The first listing is the Kinect you should probably get; otherwise, you will also need to purchase the third listing.

You might choose to go both routes at the same time: buy the standalone sensor for your computer and buy the bundle for playing games. That's an expensive path, but it lets you keep a Kinect plugged into your computer for tinkering and always have another Kinect to use with your Xbox without having to move cords and cameras around. Newer drivers and software are becoming available to support the use of multiple Kinects simultaneously, so you might find value in having more than one at your disposal.

Separating a Kinect from an Xbox

So, you already have an Xbox? Awesome. Okay, now you need to borrow the Kinect from your Xbox and bring it over to a computer. You'll probably want to ask permission from whomever's Kinect you are using before you proceed. I'm sure they'll miss it! Tell them you'll give it back after you show them all the cool stuff you can do with a Kinect on a computer once you get through Chapter 3. They'll thank you!

Disconnecting the Kinect from a late model Xbox is very straightforward. Simply locate the Kinect, follow the cord to the back of your Xbox, and pull it out. Done. Now, you'll just need the Kinect AC adapter and you'll be ready to move on to downloading and installing software.

If you've got a Kinect successfully hooked up to an early model Xbox, that's great news—it means you've got all the parts necessary to take the sensor and plug it into your computer. To disconnect your Kinect from an older model Xbox, you'll be removing two components—the Kinect sensor itself, and the attached cable that leads to the Xbox and AC wall outlet (Figure 1-3). Once you've disconnected those two things, you are all set.

Figure 1-3. *Unplugging the Kinect and AC adapter from an early model Xbox game console (Photo courtesy Microsoft)*

Making Sure You Have the AC Adapter

If you have a new model Xbox with a Kinect, it's possible that they were purchased as a bundle. If that's the case, then you probably don't yet own the adapter cable necessary to make the Kinect work on a computer. Unfortunately, now you'll have to purchase the AC adapter cable before you can continue. The third item in Figure 1-2 shows the product information for the adapter as it should appear on Amazon.com. Figure 1-4 shows a better image of the cable itself.

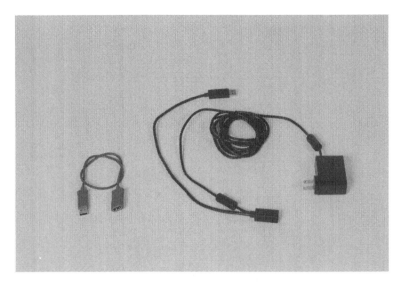

Figure 1-4. *Kinect USB extender on the left for newer XBox syststems, and the Kinect power adapter on the right.*

The power adapter cable is required for two reasons. First, the Kinect requires more power than a standard USB port can deliver, probably because of all of the components it has inside, such as a motor, a number of sensors, and a fan to push air through the device for cooling. The special USB port on the late model Xbox can deliver this extra power, but because your computer can't, you have to compensate for that by plugging the Kinect into an electrical outlet with the AC adapter provided on the cable. This need for an adapter cable is frustrating if you want to go mobile with the Kinect and a laptop—you'll need a 12-volt battery and some careful modification to get past that problem.

The second reason you need the adapter cable is that the cord on the Kinect uses a proprietary, Xbox-only USB connector. This is frustrating, I know. The AC adapter cable has a port that accepts this special USB shape on one end and turns it into a standard USB connector on the other. The older Xbox systems have a standard USB port, which is why they also require an adapter cable to be compatible with the Kinect. When Microsoft launches a version of Windows with Kinect support built-in, they may introduce a lower-power version of the Kinect for use with computers that doesn't require this pesky AC adapter attachment.

Inspecting the Kinect, Part by Part

Now that you've acquired a Kinect, let's take a closer look at all the parts. Figure 1-5 shows all the items in the box from a standalone, Kinect Sensor purchase. The only ones you need to follow along with this book are the AC Adapter and the Kinect itself. You can keep the USB extender, manuals, and Kinect Adventures game disc in the box, as you may need them if you have or plan to get an Xbox.

Before you throw away that box, you should know that it functions as a handy way to store and transport the bulky and oddly shaped Kinect. The device is pretty rugged; very few are returned defective or broken, and they can take a beating. However, the original box is a popular way for people to bring the sensor to and from meetups and hackathons in NYC. The foam inside is shaped perfectly to hold the Kinect, making the box a simple, portable container, so you might want to hang on to it just in case.

Figure 1-5. Contents of standalone Kinect sensor box: Manual, Kinect Adventures! game disc, the Kinect itself, AC adapter, and special USB extender.

Now, let's take a look at the inputs and outputs you'll be able to take advantage of in applications and when building your own projects or products. Being able to identify all the components on the outside of the device (Figure 1-6) will be very helpful going forward. There's a lot going on, and many people aren't quite sure which part does what. After reading through this section, you'll know the function of every part and be able to apply that knowledge to your advantage.

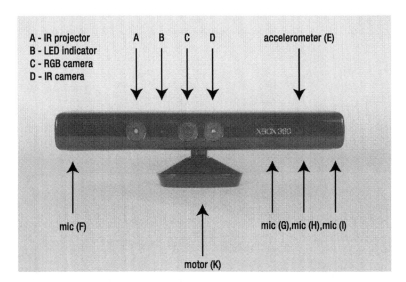

A - IR projector
B - LED indicator
C - RGB camera
D - IR camera

A B C D   accelerometer (E)

mic (F)   mic (G),mic (H),mic (I)

motor (K)

Figure 1-6. Kinect external component identification— Output: A) IR (infrared) structured-light laser projector, B) LED indicator, and K) motor to control tilt-in base. Input: F-I) Four microphones, C-D) two cameras (RGB and IR), and E) one accelerometer

There are two basic ideas when working with hardware, and with technology in general, that are really important: input and output. Input is information that comes into a system from an external source, and output is information that goes out from a system. I learned about inputs and outputs by hooking up stereos, TVs, and VCRs as a kid. An input to a stereo might be through a microphone or an iPod, whereas an output could be to a speaker or amplifier. Many devices, such as an amplifier, can both receive input and send output. The Kinect has sensors that act as inputs, reading (or sampling) information in space about the physical environment in front of it. The Kinect also has actuators (outputs) that allow it to write or act upon the physical space by changing it in different ways.

There are four microphones on the Kinect—that's right, four! That's not just stereo; it's actually quadraphonic sound. Combined with advanced digital signal processing in software, these four mics can be used to do remarkable things. In combination, these four audio inputs can work to filter out background noise and detect the relative position of anyone speaking within a room. Looking at the Kinect head on, there are three adjacent mics on the right side, just below the "XBOX 360" label (Figure 1-6, G-I). A fourth microphone is on the left side (Figure 1-6, F). Microsoft's official Kinect SDK (Software Development Kit) is the first to reveal how to access the microphones, although other drivers are expected to provide access to this hardware in the future.

The Kinect kind of looks like a huge, clunky old webcam, which is fitting because there's actually a standard webcam built right into the middle of it (Figure 1-6, C). Next to it is an infrared camera, which is a bit more exotic than a standard webcam. Equally interesting, if not downright mysterious, is the 3-axis accelerometer inside the device, behind the "XBOX 360" label. Most people didn't expect the Kinect to contain such a sensor, which is more common in devices designed to be held in your hand, such as a mobile phone or the Nintendo Wii controller.

Now, for the outputs. You may have heard that the Kinect has a laser in it—it's true. You can see it glowing red (Figure 1-6, A) when the Kinect is plugged in, even though the light the projector emits is in the infrared spectrum and mostly invisible. It works in combination with the infrared camera on the unit (Figure 1-6, D) to derive the exact position in space of everything in the room it occupies. The other light-based output is the LED indicator (Figure 1-6, B). It's not easily accessible from frameworks such as OpenNI; however, if you have a project that would benefit from feedback through the hardware, this may be of interest to you. It could be an ideal way for the application to alert a user that something is happening without requiring a screen. For example, in the 3D capture tool MatterPort, the user picks up the Kinect and walks around the room—away from the computer—to photograph objects. An audible beep from the computer lets the user know once a particular view has been adequately analyzed. This beep could be accompanied by a flicker of the LED light on the unit as an additional cue, so the user doesn't have to be looking at the screen to register it.

Finally, the Kinect has the functional opposite of a sensor, called an actuator, in the form of a small motor driving gears that pitch the tilt of the camera 30 degrees up or down. This could be put to novel use in the applications you build. For example, by sweeping the device and its sensor elements up and down through space, the Kinect can be used to capture high-resolution scans of the environment around it. If you want to mount a Kinect to a robot, the motor could provide the mechanical up-and-down motion of the camera. Additionally, if you employ face or body tracking, you can adjust the position of the camera to adapt when a person moves out of the field of view.

Now that we have identified all of the Kinect hardware, let's put it to use with software. You'll have a chance to see the imagery that comes from the RGB camera, as well as the depth image computed from the infrared projector and camera combination.

KINECT TEARDOWN!

Interested in an insider view of the Kinect? The website iFixit has put together a writeup and a video that take you through a tear-down of the Kinect device.

Read the teardown article at: http://www.ifixit.com/Teardown/Microsoft-Kinect-Teardown/4066/

Watch the teardown video at: http://www.ifixit.com/blog/blog/2010/11/05/kinect-teardown-video/

Please don't try it at home! Don't risk your own device. If you're curious about what's inside, visit iFixit.com.

Downloading and Installing Software

The first time I plugged my Kinect into a computer to see how it worked, I used the software you'll install in this section. That software is RGBDemo, and I still reach for it whenever I want to demonstrate what the Kinect is capable of and how it is different from a standard webcam. RGB stands for red, green and blue—the colors the webcam in the middle of the Kinect can see. The D in Demo also stands for depth, which the IR projector and IR camera generate with the help of a structured-light chip from a company called PrimeSense. Who is PrimeSense?

PrimeSense is the Israeli company whose hardware reference design and structured-light decoding chip are at the heart of the Kinect's volumetric 3D camera system. This was a surprise to many who had tracked the evolution of the Kinect (originally code-named Project Natal), as many thought Microsoft would use the intellectual property of the two time-of-flight 3D sensor companies they had recently acquired—3DV Systems and Canesta. Following the lead of the OpenKinect project, PrimeSense went on to help found OpenNI in an effort to put the best tools in the hands of developers. OpenNI has launched the first major store offering PC applications that make use of volumetric cameras such as those in the Kinect with the debut of Arena, which will be covered in more detail in Chapter 3.

While those approaching the Kinect from a natural user-interface perspective see the Kinect as a 3D gesture-recognition device, people from engineering and robotics backgrounds refer to this particular aspect of the Kinect's hardware as an RGBD sensor. RGBDemo is intended to provide a demonstration of how the Kinect performs as an RGBD sensor in applications such as machine vision and 3D reconstruction—hence, the name RGBDemo. It's the most straightforward way to get a look at the low-level data from the Kinect on both Mac and Windows machines.

Why do you need to download software if the Kinect "just works" on your Xbox? Well, if you plugged your Kinect into a computer without installing some drivers and applications that know how to talk to the Kinect, nothing would happen! So, while I know you must be eager to get going, please wait until you carefully go through the steps in order before plugging in your Kinect. Some of these steps need to be carried out in a very specific order. Please follow along!

First, you'll need to go on the Web and download RGBDemo, a powerful suite of open-source software written by Nicolas Burrus to provide a toolkit that others can use to write programs and a means for noncoders to see what the Kinect data really looks like. If you're on Windows, then you'll install three included drivers from OpenNI that help RGBDemo make better sense of the data from the Kinect. The RGBD-viewer application included with the software will show you the kind of imagery the Kinect can see and the unique ways in which it does so—this will be how we test that you've got everything hooked up correctly.

Nicolas Burrus, originally from Paris, explores the use of depth sensing cameras like the one in the Kinect for his postdoctoral research in computer vision at the robotics lab of Carlos III University of Madrid (`http://roboticslab.uc3m.es/`). Many thanks are owed to Nicolas for being the first to package up a simple executable program anyone can use with the Kinect on their computer, the same month the Kinect debuted. For coders, the collection of source code and related machine vision libraries he assembled for RGBDemo helped many people get started building applications. For less technical people, RGBDemo provided a means to see the Kinect data for the first time without having to write any code. Burrus and his partner, Nicolas Tisserand, have since formed a company called manctl (`http://manctl.com`) to further innovate around Kinect-related technology. Let's take a look at how to get started with RGBDemo.

Finding the Correct Version of RGBDemo

First, you need to find the correct version of RGBDemo for your operating system. Open up a web browser and go to `http://labs.manctl.com/rgbdemo` in order to pull up the latest information about the software project (Figure 1-7). Nicolas updates the codebase regularly, and you'll need to pick the most recent version that works on your system. As of this writing, v0.6.1 is the latest version that works for Windows and Intel Mac OS X Snow Leopard. As of this writing, the RGBDemo project has just been given a home on the manctl web site, so be aware that its appearance may have changed by the time you visit.

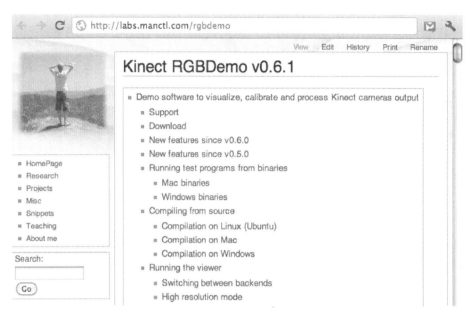

Figure 1-7. RGBDemo project web page

RGBDemo is an open-source software project. Delightfully, it therefore includes not only an application ready to run as a "binary executable," but the source code of its composition as well. Open-source projects such as this one are valuable: If you find a problem with the software or want to extend it in a new way, you have the recipe to cook your own version from the original instructions, which you can then compile into your own improved "binary executable" application. Many open-source projects come with only the source code and nothing you can use without knowing how to compile programs. That's not much fun if you aren't that technical. RGBDemo is wonderful because it's ready to run with an executable binary file, in addition to letting you see how it was constructed.

Now, let's jump to the binary software that can run on your operating system. To do that, the following material is split up into different instructions for Windows and Mac users. After the download and installation, we'll meet up once again in the "Testing Your Kinect" section, where we'll launch RGBDemo and tinker around to make sure everything is working.

Downloading and Installing RGBDemo for Windows

Depending on which version of Windows you are using—XP, Vista, or Windows 7—your experience with the details in this section may vary. These instructions address some of the hangups you could face when downloading and installing on Vista that you might not experience on XP or Windows 7. You can just skip the explanations of those problems if you don't run into them, but they're included so we don't leave any of the less advanced readers behind. This process can be tedious on Windows, compared to the much simpler Mac installation.

Downloading the Binaries

Enough talk—let's get that software! On the RGBDemo web page, click the `Windows binaries` download link, as shown in Figure 1-8. The page will jump to a line that contains a link to a file called `RGBDemo-0.6.1rc1-Win32.zip` (Figure 1-9). Before you click that download link, you'll need to carefully carry out two steps in sequence.

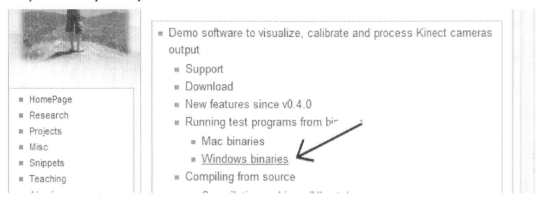

Figure 1-8. *The link for* `Windows binaries` *on the Kinect RGBDemo page*

First, I want you to select and copy the 28-character License Key, as shown in Figure 1-9. You will need to use this in a moment and, if you copy it to your clipboard now, you will be able to paste it in the next step without having to come back to this page and hunt for it. This long string of letters, numbers, and symbols is a license to use the PrimeSense NITE middleware with the OpenNI framework.

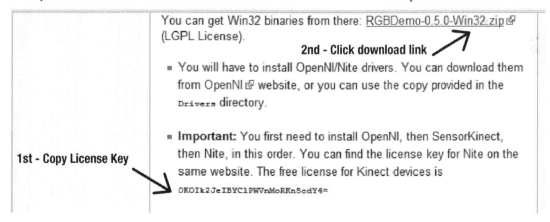

Figure 1-9. *Screen showing the License Key and the download link for the RGBDemo* `ZIP` *file*

Great! Now, let's click the link at the top of the screen (Figure 1-9) to download the `RGBDemo-0.6.1rc1-Win32.zip` compressed file.

Bam! What just happened? Your browser is now at another site called SourceForge (Figure 1-10), which hosts this popular file. Don't be alarmed when the RGBDemo software starts to download automatically. Or, you may see a dialog box prompting you to select a save location for the file. The compressed file is over 60MB in size and could take a bit of time to download depending on the speed of your Internet connection.

Figure 1-10. Downloading from SourceForge

You may need to respond to an alert that says something like `This type of file can harm your computer. Are you sure you want to download RGBDemo-0.6.1rc1-Win32.zip?` Answer affirmatively, and when `RGBDemo-0.6.1rc1-Win32.zip` is finished downloading, double-click the `ZIP` file to see the `Extract all files` window (Figure 1-11). Simply click the icon for the RGBDemo folder and drag it out of the window and over to your desktop to extract it there.

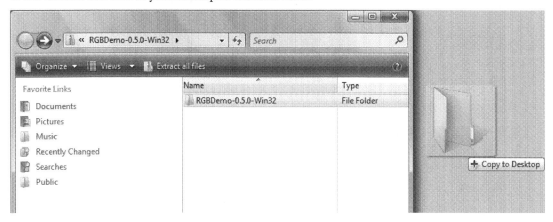

Figure 1-11. Dragging the RGBDemo folder to the desktop

You may be prompted with a Windows Security Warning asking `Are you sure you want to copy and move files to this folder?` Click Yes. Windows will copy the folder and all its files over to the desktop. Once it has finished, open the folder on your desktop and you'll see a listing of all the files and folders inside the directory (Figure 1-12).

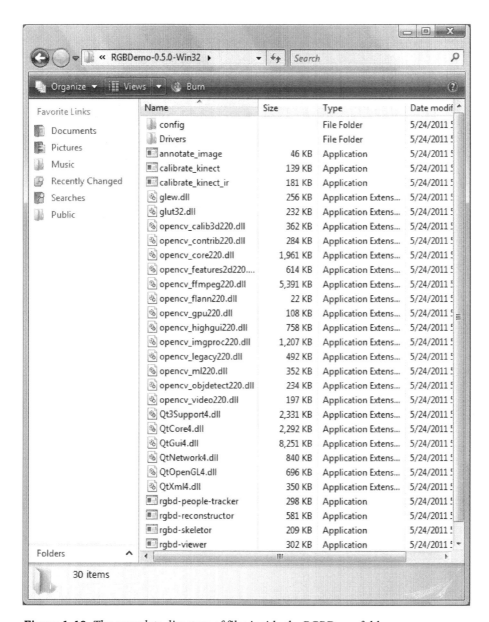

Figure 1-12. *The complete directory of files inside the RGBDemo folder*

Now, go into the directory labeled **Drivers**. Once you are in the **Drivers** directory, you will see a list of three **MSI** installation files—don't click any, yet! You'll need to install them in a very critical order (Figure 1-13), so pay attention and follow along, please. Perform the installation in the following order:

1.   OpenNI-**Win32**

2. `SensorKinect-Win-OpenSource32`

3. `NITE-Win32`

Notice that the order in which the files are listed in the directory as shown in Figure 1-13 won't necessarily match the proper installation order. So be careful! Pay attention to the order as I describe it.

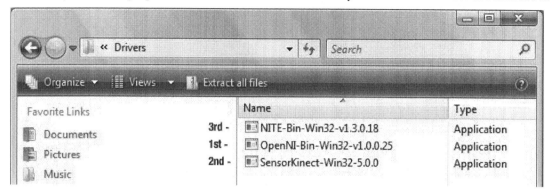

Figure 1-13. *Critical order of driver installation: 1.) OpenNI- Win32, 2.) SensorKinect-Win-OpenSource32, 3.) NITE- Win32*

First, you need to install OpenNI (Figure 1-14). This is a framework for "natural interface" technology that allows modules for different hardware and software to talk with each other. Next, you'll install SensorKinect (Figure 1-16), a device module that registers the Kinect with OpenNI so it can read its sensor data. Finally, you'll install NITE (Figure 1-17), a "middleware" module that processes the volumetric data coming from the Kinect and derives a map of a person's skeletal structure that can be used by an application, controlling gestures and other interactivity.

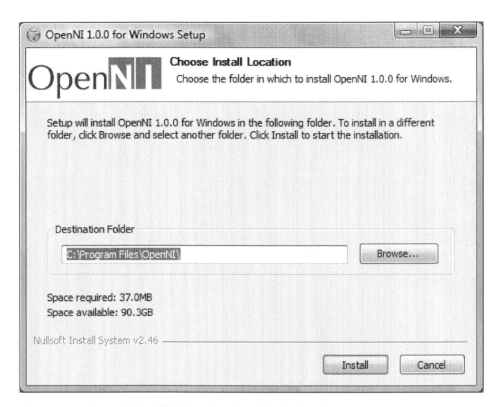

Figure 1-14. OpenNI install dialog showing default destination

Installing OpenNI

Double-click the `OpenNI-Win32` file to start the installer. Depending on your settings and which version of Windows you are using, you might get a Windows Security Warning (Figure 1-15, top). Just respond in the affirmative—in this case, `Install`. Don't worry, all of the software you are instructed to download in this book are from safe sources. In the OpenNI setup application, you can accept the default path, `C:\Program Files\OpenNI`, click `Install`, and close the window once it's finished.

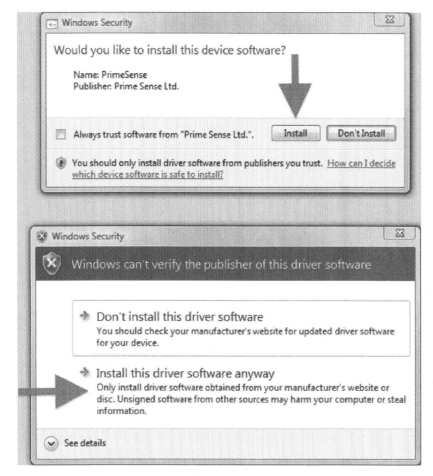

Figure 1-15. *Windows Security Warnings—It's okay to trust software from PrimeSense Ltd; choose*
`Install`.

Installing SensorKinect

Next, launch the `SensorKinect-Win-OpenSource32` setup application and be sure that both `OpenNI` and
`Sensor` are checked in the component selection dialog box (Figure 1-16). Near the end of the installation,
you may see another Windows Security Warning (Figure 1-15, bottom)—click `Install this driver`
`software anyway`, then close the window when the process has completed.

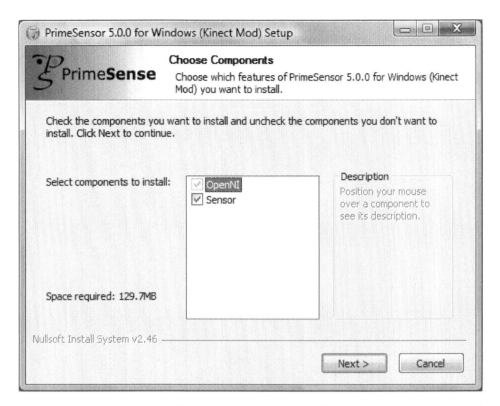

Figure 1-16. Component install choices—Make sure both OpenNI and Sensor are checked

Installing PrimeSense NITE

Finally, install the last driver by launching the `NITE- Win32` setup application. Agree to the license agreement, keep the default installation path as `C:\Program Files\Prime Sense\NITE\`, and click `Install`. In the next step, you'll be prompted for a license key (Figure 1-17). Paste in the string of 28 characters that you copied from the RGBDemo download page (Figure 1-9) and hit `Install`. It's normal for a couple of command prompt windows to open and close by themselves during this step, so don't be alarmed.

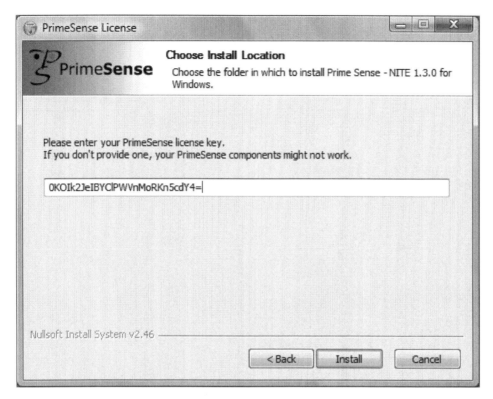

Figure 1-17. PrimeSense prompt for NITE license key—0KOIk2JeIBYClPWVnMoRKn5cdY4=

Plugging in the Kinect

Congratulations! You are done installing. Now, for the fun part—you are ready to plug the Kinect into your computer. Refer back to Figure 1-4 for a visual overview of the cords involved in this next series of steps. Take the special male USB plug directly on the Kinect and plug it into the female USB connector on the AC adapter cable. Plug the AC adapter into a wall outlet, and then plug the standard USB connector into a USB port on your computer. This should look something like Figure 1-3 but instead of unplugging from an Xbox you are plugging into your computer. You may see the Kinect's LED indicator turn on or blink. Now, go ahead and point the Kinect at yourself from a distance of about two feet.

Once you have plugged in the Kinect, you may see various system notifications (Figure 1-18, bottom) about driver software installation. Depending on your system configuration, you may see individual notifications for the motor, cameras, and Xbox NUI Audio. This could take a while, so please be patient. Windows may be unable to find the audio drivers because these sensor drivers are only for the PrimeSense-related components of the Kinect (Figure 1-18, top). When Microsoft licensed the design, they added their own array of four microphones (See F-I in Figure 1-6) on top of the PrimeSense reference specification. Microsoft has yet to distribute third-party drivers for the audio components on Windows; however, they provide full audio support in their official SDK. Therefore, if prompted to locate audio drivers, select the choice labeled `Don't show this message again for this device` and don't worry about Windows not finding the `Xbox NUI Audio` device (Figure 1-18, top)—this is normal.

18

Figure 1-18. *Xbox NUI Audio driver not found message and system tray notification*

If you are running Windows Vista, you will probably be prompted to restart; go ahead and do that. When you return to Windows, it will show a screen saying it is configuring updates and warn you not to turn off your computer. It could take a while depending on your system. When it's done, you'll finally be able to tinker around with the Kinect on your computer!

Navigate to the RGBDemo folder on your desktop and launch the `rgbd-viewer` application (Figure 1-12, last item in directory). A black command prompt window will appear with the message `Setting resolution to VGA`. This is normal and should be followed by the graphical user interface window of RGBDemo (Figure 1-21, later in the chapter).

Now, skip to the "Testing your Kinect" section, as the following pages explain the download and installation process for Mac OS X. If you're curious, take a look at the process as described in this section for Apple computer users.

Downloading and Installing RGBDemo for Mac OS X

RGBDemo is available for the Intel-based Macs and requires Snow Leopard or Lion. Unfortunately, PowerPC-based machines are not supported. Navigate to the RGBDemo site at `http://labs.manctl.com/rgbdemo` and locate the `Mac Binaries` link.

The file is hosted at SourceForge, and will download automatically, as pictured in Figure 1-19. You may need to confirm by clicking Yes in response to a message such as This type of file can harm your computer. Are you sure you want to download RGBDemo-0.6.1-Darwin.dmg? There's nothing in RGBDemo that will harm your computer, so don't worry.

Once the file has finished downloading, click it so it will expand into a disk image. The resulting disk image (Figure 1-19, bottom) will contain two folders. Drag the RGBDemo folder onto the Applications folder. Then, navigate to the Applications folder, find RGBDemo, and navigate into it. Once inside, you'll see a listing of all the files and folders in that directory (Figure 1-20). It's that simple.

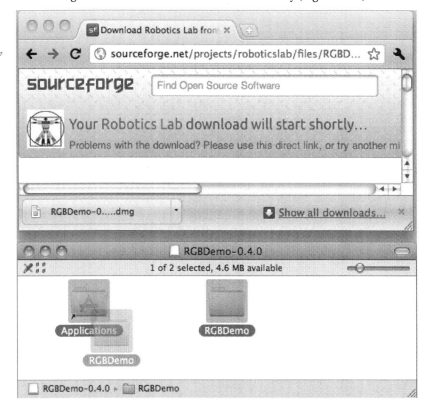

Figure 1-19. *RGBDemo-0.6.1-Darwin.dmg* *download and resulting disk image containing RGBDemo folder and link to Applications*

Congratulations! You are done installing. Now, for the fun part—you are ready to plug the Kinect into your computer. Refer to Figure 1-4 for a visual overview of the cords used in this next series of steps. Take the special male USB plug on the Kinect and plug it into the female USB connector on the AC adapter cable. Plug the AC adapter into a wall outlet, and then plug the standard USB connector into a USB port on your computer. This should look something like Figure 1-3, but instead of unplugging from an Xbox, you are plugging into your computer. You should see the Kinect's LED indicator turn on or blink.

Now, point the Kinect at yourself from a distance of about two feet. Let's launch the rgbd-viewer application as shown in Figure 1-20. You are ready to test the Kinect on yourself! You should see the

RGBDemo user interface as pictured in Figure 1-21. This is the end of the section on downloading and installing RGBDemo for Mac OS X. The rest of this chapter applies for both Windows and Apple computers. Well done!

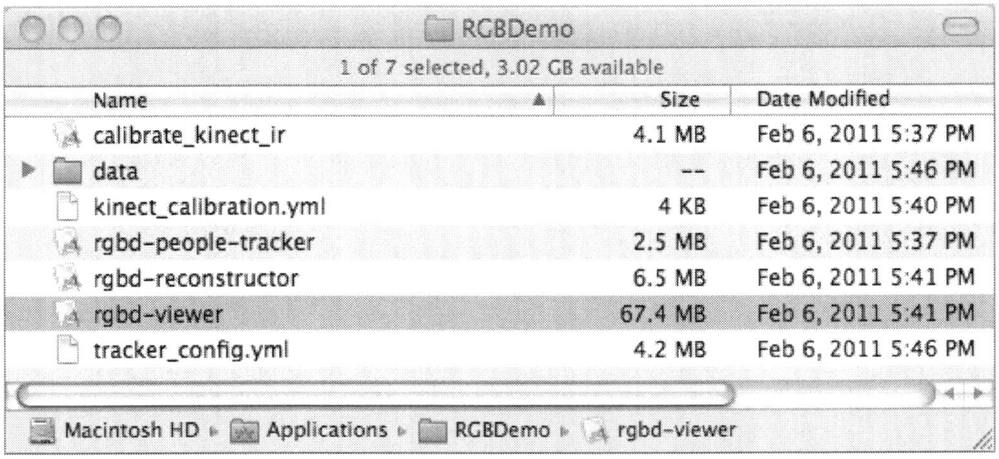

Figure 1-20. The complete directory of files in the RGBDemo folder, with the `rgbd-viewer` application selected

Testing your Kinect

Are you ready to see yourself in volumetric 3D?! Okay, if you've followed the steps successfully, you should be looking at yourself like I am in Figure 1-21. This colorful, realtime view of you looks like a thermal camera image from a science fiction movie, but that's where the similarity ends.

Figure 1-21. *RGBD Capture window in* `rgbd-viewer` *application. Main image shows merged depth range image mapped to color values representing distance from sensor. Upper right image shows* `Color Image` *stream from RGB camera.* `3D View` *and* `Filters` *options are shown in the* `Show` *dropdown menu. Distance value for each pixel is shown in upper middle* `Distance at...` *status corresponding to location of mouse pointer on depth range image.*

Instead of showing different colors representing a range of temperatures like a thermal camera, the Kinect shows different colors for a range of distances from the camera. These colors are arbitrary—some other drivers display the depth image as a grayscale range, instead. You can see the exact distance in meters of any pixel, or picture element, in the image from the camera by moving your mouse over any part of the colored image of yourself. Look just above and to the right of the depth image and you'll see a readout such as `Distance at (0,414) = 0.000 m` in Figure 1-21. Try rolling your pointer around and see how far different things in your environment are from the camera. The readout is calibrated in meters, not feet, but you can find a converter online.

Take a moment to jump around in front of the camera and observe how the depth image reflects your movements in space. Pick up the Kinect and point it at the walls and floor around you, and note the change in color corresponding to the change in distance of these objects from the device. All of the depth data about the scene can be sent to the programs you write, and the other chapters in this book will go into detail about how that works. Additionally, you'll learn about the fundamentals of people and skeleton tracking in Chapter 2. For now, we'll just focus on the basics of the data and imagery coming out of the Kinect without any sophisticated middleware.

It's a pretty simple idea—every pixel in the image has a location in space as measured from the camera. No other consumer camera has ever had the Kinect's ability to measure space. This is the raw functionality of a "depth sensor", which has been used in robotics and engineering for years. With just the depth sensor, as well as skeletal tracking middleware and other tracking methods we'll look at later, software developers can create simple "natural interface" software that makes it easier to interact with machines without touching them. It's pretty cool—but what we'll do next shows how, with the help of the right software, the Kinect breaks away from just depth sensing to usher in a whole new class of equipment, becoming the first consumer-grade volumetric 3D camera, or voxelcam for short.

In Figure 1-21, you can see a normal webcam view of yourself in the upper right corner labeled `Color Image`. The signal is coming from the visible light camera sensor behind the lens in the middle of the Kinect (Figure 1-6, C). What you are looking at in the `Color Image` window is a live video stream of visible light, organized on your screen in the same way that still pictures and video have been displayed on screens since the dawn of television—through a 2D table of picture elements, or pixels. Like a spreadsheet with rows and columns of light samples, and a color value for each cell in the table, these elements are stitched together to form a mosaic on the screen. Note that by default the `Intensity Image` and the `Amplitude Image` in the lower right of the window in Figure 1-21 are turned off. Nothing is wrong with your setup if you don't see anything in that area.

Now, you'll add another dimension to the camera image with the help of the depth range image data. Breaking from all traditional photography and video as we've known it, we can now assign each picture element a location in 3D space that reflects the position of the original surface from which it was sampled (Figure 1-22). For every pixel in the depth image, we can extract three dimensions: its distance from the camera (z), its vertical position in a column of the image table (y), and its horizontal position in a row of the image table (x).

Figure 1-22. RGBDemo 3D View—synthetic camera in alignment with actual camera by default

These floating points, or "pixels in space", are hard to imagine. They have no color or texture of their own. They are merely used to indicate the presence of something that is reflecting the infrared laser pattern. To provide a more concrete way of understanding these points in space, we'll move from the 2D metaphor of a spreadsheet to a 3D metaphor of a Rubik's cube. Imagine each point as having a volume of its own as represented by a single cube within the larger Rubik's cube. An individual cubic volume element, or voxel, from this larger 3D array of cubes acts as a container for information, with an address in x, y, and z coordinates designating a chunk of physical space in the scene. That means we can merge the picture elements from the webcam with the voxels from the Depth Cam to build a volumetric cubic space that has both depth and color. This process assembles a live cloud of colored voxels in 3D space that reconstruct the surface shape and appearance of objects in front of the Kinect (Figure 1-22). Unlike 2D computer vision technology, such as the Playstation Move or Nintendo Wii, this ability to parse the voxel map of a scene with depth information is fundamental to understanding the power of the Kinect and how you can work with it.

Are you ready to get voxelated? Okay, to see yourself in volumetric 3D, first click Show from the menu bar in the RGBD Capture window, and then select 3D View. A new window will pop up labeled 3D View (Figure 1-22). You're not quite there yet—at this point you should see yourself like you would on a normal webcam, but with some rough edges around your head and other objects. Here's the fun part: click on yourself and drag. Now, that's what you've been waiting for (Figure 1-23)!

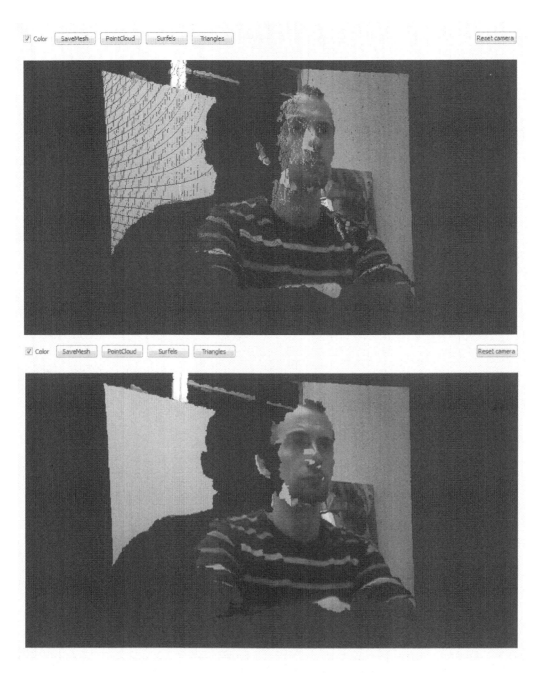

Figure 1-23. *3D View with synthetic camera rotated slightly to the left. Top view shows default* PointCloud *render mode, bottom view shows* Triangles *render mode*

What you are looking at is a "synthetic camera" image in volumetric space. The synthetic camera isn't really there—its image is derived from peering at the floating volume elements in space from a different angle than that at which they were originally sampled. You can take this synthetic camera and spin it in any direction to look at the voxel data from any angle. Figure 1-24, for example, shows the image rotated 90 degrees.

Since you are using only a single camera, the image will start to look more incomplete if you try to peer behind objects facing it, and you can extrapolate this from Figure 1-24. It's possible to arrange a number of voxelcams in a space in order to build a more complete scene. Both the Microsoft Kinect SDK and OpenNI framework actually include support for interfacing with multiple Kinects simultaneously. Therefore, if you wanted to create an application that filled in imagery gaps from multiple angles, it is possible to write software to do that. This single, comprehensive volumetric view of a space could be observed from infinite perspectives, all positioned in real time interactively during playback with synthetic cameras that map to the direction a viewer is looking.

Once people catch on to what this technology can really do, there will be an increased demand for more truly immersive experiences. As volumetric sensor arrays become more common to meet this demand, the possibilities of what can be created from this technology grow even more limitless. The Kinect is the tip of the iceberg. Welcome to the volumetric age!

These buckets of information can be rendered in different ways. The default method for 3D View is just a cloud of pixels in space, also called a point cloud (Figure 1-23, top). This view has lots of holes in it, as you can see. You can zoom in to see the points even closer—the pattern they display reflects the structured-light dot pattern invisibly cascading over you from the IR projector.

Since we don't have multiple Kinects to fill in all the cracks of this synthetic camera image just yet, let's use the magic of polygons to render this information in a way we are more accustomed to seeing. Select the button in the upper right section of the 3D View screen (Figure 1-23) labeled `Triangles`, located to the right of the `PointCloud` and `Surfels` buttons. This will create a mesh of triangle-shaped polygons that connect the dots and allow the visible light image data more surface area to display. Notice the difference between point cloud view and triangle view (Figure 1-23, bottom). The ability to create this kind of 3D imagery was only within reach of academic, entertainment, and military institutions that could afford a price tag in the US$15,000 range only a few years ago.

Figure 1-24. *RGBDemo 3D View showing volumetric 3D synthetic camera perspective magically rotating 90 degrees perpendicular to the physical Kinect*

You'll notice the big hole in the image "behind" where you are sitting – that's your shadow! Your shape is silhouetted because you are blocking the IR projector from placing measurable light on the wall behind you. It may not look like much, since this is a very rudimentary use of the technology, but you can get an idea of where this capability is leading when you check out Microsoft Research's KinectFusion project for realtime dynamic 3D surface reconstruction. This ability to reconstruct the physical world in digital space is a major theme at Microsoft, and simple applications that have you "digitize your world" can be found in the Fun Labs minigames available from Xbox Live.

▨ **Note** Learn more about the the KinectFusion project at the following URL: http://research.microsoft.com/en-us/projects/surfacerecon/

While most people only see the Kinect as a natural interface 3D gesture recognition device, it is important to understand the imaging data that body-tracking software and other features are built upon. The Kinect's ability to gather spatial information is the heart of its unique hardware functionality. Some of the great "hacks" seen on YouTube work with just this raw data and don't even go to the level of using the Kinect for gesture recognition. Microsoft Research's debut of KinectFusion (Figure 1-25) at SIGGRAPH 2011, the leading industry conference for graphics experts, shocked many in the tech world. Previously, the volumetric video output from the Kinect was panned as too low quality to be useful. KinectFusion's high-resolution, realtime, photorealistic reconstruction of people and objects, even with a shaky camera, demonstrated that a persistent model of an entire scene could be stored and updated rapidly to fill in missing detail behind the view of the camera.

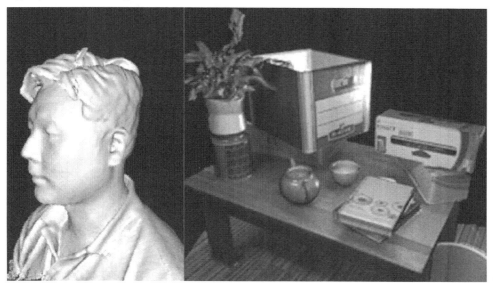

Figure 1-25. *KinectFusion showing realtime reconstruction of person in 3D (left) and photorealistic texture map model with lighting effects (right). Courtesy Microsoft Research.*

It's likely that what you've glimpsed in this chapter, seeing yourself in live volumetric 3D video, will play a key part in shaping screen-based entertainment and virtual presence in the future. Instead of using instant messaging or Skype as we know it, you could be communicating with friends, family, and colleagues by "instant personing" them into your room with you. Receiving full 3D data of their bodies, you may be able to tilt your head and look around them as if they were there, something not possible with today's 2D cameras. Expect a whole class of applications that invite you to "digitize" people and objects in your home and bring them into a game or novel application. Now, you know what the real Kinect data looks like and have a perspective on the kind of experiences that are possible in the not-too-distant future. The rest of the book will go into more detail on how body-tracking points extracted from this "voxelated" physical information can be used today to design applications with natural, gestural interfaces.

CHAPTER 2

Behind the Technology

In this chapter, we'll demystify the underlying technology behind Kinect. You'll learn about the principles of depth–sensing imagers, discover alternatives to Kinect that are available through other manufacturers, and understand the general data output that all of these devices offer to your potential applications. You can create applications through various drivers, processing libraries, and application development environments. You'll be exposed to new language that is used to describe working with depth and natural interface technology and be provided with a mental framework for relating these new ideas to ones you're already familiar with from 2D technology.

One of the challenges of working with new technology is that the concepts behind it have not yet worked their way into common knowledge or become household names. Because Kinect was designed as a video game controller that can provide a "natural interface" for gaming, much of the literature on its development focuses on its application as a "mouse/remote/game controller replacement" input device for the living room. This is an emerging field, and a number of hardware and software manufacturers have designed their own systems to accomplish this, albeit in slightly different ways. As a result, there are disparities in the language used by people and companies from different backgrounds who are developing this technology for different environments. In some cases, there is not even a well–defined vocabulary that describes how aspects of this technology work when they are applied outside the boundaries of a "natural interface."

The problem is that since Kinect was liberated from its attachment to the Xbox, many of the most interesting "hacks" have used the device in ways that were never intended by the manufacturers. Therefore, as concepts and techniques once locked away in academic research or industrial applications make their way into the public consciousness—through YouTube videos and other popular media— there is a need to come up with descriptions of technology for conversational use by general audiences. In order to explain how to use these new technologies as designed, while still addressing the imaginative off–label uses that are driving innovation, liberties must be taken to bend "expert" terminology in order to provide a more open–ended view of the technology's possibilities.

As we move away from conventions of imaging and input systems based on 2D principles—such as a webcam and a mouse—to those based on 3D systems such as Kinect, we will identify principles that provide a concrete reference between the two dimensions. After that, we will look at the complete Kinect "stack," from hardware to software, in order to explain how this technology works.

Understanding the Technology Stack

The technology stack is a way of describing the relationship between the components that make up a hardware and software solution. The scope of the stack can be adjusted to the context of what is being described. Using a personal computer as an example, we can identify a hardware manufacturer (HP), an operating system (Windows 7), and an application that users can run (Google Chrome). Using web applications as an example, we can look at the server operating system (Linux), the web server software

(Apache), the database software (MySQL), and the web scripting language (PHP). The stack provides a perspective on the complete system design and the chosen components in combination, or as elements that can be swapped in and out. There are so many ways to use Kinect and its revolutionary inexpensive 3D depth sensor that people may choose different technology stacks depending on how they wish to utilize the technology. This book is primarily about ways to use Kinect as way of enabling natural interface experiences; others may use it for filmmaking, 3D reconstruction of objects and environments, or providing a machine vision system for a new class of affordable robotics.

Originally, the only way to develop Kinect applications (apps) was to use a $10,000 Xbox Development Kit (XDK) supplied by Microsoft to its partners at high–level studios so they could design applications exclusively for the Xbox system (Figure 2-1, left). That changed dramatically only days after Kinect's retail release – software drivers interpreted the signal coming from Kinect's USB port, which was then written and released as open source software on the Internet. Suddenly, with the aid of the "libfreenect" drivers, also known as "OpenKinect," anyone could develop their own apps using the Kinect sensor, free of charge. These drivers access raw data from various Kinect sensors, but don't provide a higher-level framework for making sense of the data in a natural interface–based development environment. That didn't stop curious and creative programmers from producing remarkable applications, also known as "hacks," that explored the possibilities of Kinect technology beyond gaming (Figure 2-1, right).

Figure 2-1. Original Microsoft Xbox Kinect stack vs. OpenKinect/libfreenect stack

Once unofficial Kinect apps began to gather media attention and online buzz, the companies that were previously designing software to enable the development of natural interface–based applications took notice. PrimeSense, the company that developed the enabling technology behind the structured light depth sensor inside Kinect, responded by spearheading the OpenNI initiative with a number of other industry leaders – a driver framework that allows interoperability between any depth–sensing hardware and the related software, which enables the creation of natural interface applications.

This gave developers another option for Kinect development – for the first time, they had access to a driver framework that would not require them to consider a particular manufacturer or the implementation of the depth–sensing hardware. Additionally, the OpenNI software came with tools that increased the speed of development because they solved many of the harder problems of working with raw sensor data that the libfreenect/OpenKinect drivers had not yet overcome. This software was freely available, and its source code was openly viewable. PrimeSense separately released a freely available, but closed source skeletal tracking middleware system called NITE that interprets raw data and computes simplified coordinates of body parts in order to author gesture input commands, which is similar to the technology used to create games with the Xbox Development Kit.

After OpenNI became available, Microsoft announced that a Kinect Software Development Kit for Windows would become available in the spring of 2011 for non–commercial use. Soon, companies that had spent years designing application development suites for authoring natural gesture software woke up to find a growing market demand. Previously, their systems were not easily available for download and came with licensing fees that made it too costly even to publish them on their websites. Suddenly, these companies needed to maintain relevance as thousands of developers were clamoring to create sophisticated applications – the most accessible choice was open source software. By February 2011, SoftKinectic announced the general availability of iisu, their driver system for any depth sensor as well as a development environment for body gestures, in addition to their line of DepthSense camera hardware. Omek Interactive moved to release their Beckon SDK while announcing a partnership with PMD Technologies, a time–of–flight depth camera manufacturer. GestureTek, a pioneer in body–based gesture interaction systems since the 1980s, prepared to offer their GestTrack3D SDK for general availability.

Gradually development choices have become increasingly diversified for designers and developers who are looking for tools that will help them take advantage of the possibilities offered by Kinect. Today, there are dozens of hardware and software combinations that result in novel technology stacks that can drive natural user interface experiences into the future (Figure 2-2). In the next section, we will explain the factors that determine the shape of a Kinect stack, based on the individual components.

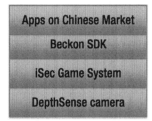 

Figure 2-2. New alternative natural interface hardware and software stacks

Hardware

A variety of devices can capture 3D imagery. Most are still expensive, which is why Kinect is such a significant breakthrough. Some devices are more appropriate for capturing still imagery, while other designs are suited for producing a high frequency of still imagery over time to generate 3D depth video. Each device captures depth information about the 3D world and stores it in ways that can reconstruct the full dimensionality of the captured 3D data. The systems may use very different operational approaches or come from different manufacturers, but the result is always data that contains some form of 3D depth information.

It can be helpful to compare the different approaches of collecting 3D imagery with the choices for collecting 2D information. Regardless of the device's operational method, a traditional camera always captures the 3D world and stores it in a 2D format. Whether it's a pinhole camera, a large format plate camera, a single lens reflex (SLR), a rangefinder, a point and shoot, or the camera in your phone, the optical systems take in light and store a negative or raw image file in flat 2D. Therefore, just as these different imaging systems exist with their own strengths and weaknesses for a particular application in 2D photography, there is a range of different ways to build 3D imaging systems as well. In depth–sensing systems, the basic premise usually includes emitting a signal, having that signal bounce off the objects in the environment, reading the signal as it returns, and computing the depth information (Figure 2-3). Regardless of the technique used, the common thread between them is the generation of a depth map image or a 3D point cloud of a scene.

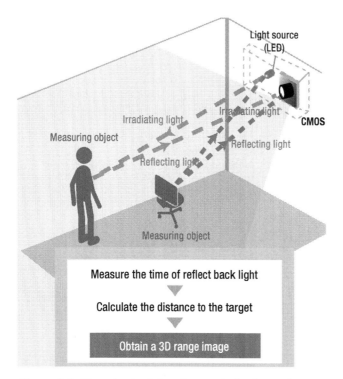

Figure 2-3. *Shared principles of most 3D depth–sensing systems. Signal is sent from the emitter, signal reflects back and is received by the sensor, calculations on returned signal are used to measure the distance to the target.*

Structured Light Camera Systems

A visible structured light approach was famously used as the basis for Radiohead's breakthrough 2008 cameraless music video, "House of Cards," from the album *In Rainbows*. With the aid of Geometric Informatics' custom system, close–up recordings of singer Tom Yorke's face were captured as point cloud data, which allowed the "synthetic camera" viewpoints to be directed in postproduction. The structured light approach was ideal for capturing the singer's detailed facial expressions since this technique can be used to capture subjects within a couple of feet. Another 3D capture technique called LIDAR, or light detection and ranging, was used to gather large–scale 3D imagery spanning hundreds of feet for renderings of buildings and roads. A US$75,000 Velodyne device with 64 synchronized spinning lasers made this imagery possible.

The data resulting from the production of the Radiohead video was made openly available through a Google code repository at `http://code.google.com/creative/radiohead/`. Kyle MacDonald explains how to recreate a setup like the one used to create the close-ups in the video at `http://www.instructables.com/id/Structured-Light-3D-Scanning/` (Figure 2-4).

Structured light scanning is the process of generating 3D depth imagery data by projecting a known signal on to a scene, such as bands of frequency, coded light, or a pattern of shapes, and observing the way this pattern is deformed as it strikes surfaces at variable distances to calculate depth range. Kinect uses an infrared structured light system, along with the ASUS WAVI Xtion and the PrimeSense reference designs. Because these systems use invisible infrared light, there is no perceivable disturbance to the environment during recording. This allows 3D capture to be unaffected by lighting conditions in the scene. In contrast, visible structured light systems work by projecting patterns on to a scene that is visible with the naked eye. Such systems provide their own illumination of the scene within the visible spectrum, which can be quite noticeable.

The visible structured light approach has some advantages. Previously, this approach was one of the less expensive options for generating depth imagery. It can produce higher resolution imagery than other approaches, such as time–of–flight cameras, at a fraction of the cost. In a visible structured light system, a projector can be used to overlay a pattern of shapes, such as lines, that are still or moving at high frequencies and bend around objects. One or more cameras are pointed at the structured light and calculations are processed on the resulting imagery to generate depth data. For example, the PR2 robot by Willow Garage uses an LED "texture" projector to overlay a pattern on the scene in front of the robot that looks like random red pixilated static. The Robot Operating System uses a narrow angle stereo camera pair that is pointed at the visible pattern to generate a 3D point cloud. Artists like Kyle MacDonald have successfully constructed visible structured light systems with off–the–shelf components (Figure 2-4) including the Sony Playstation Eye high–speed camera, DLP data projectors, and software written in Processing – an open source creative coding suite covered in Chapter 4. It is technically possible, although perhaps costly, to modify this visible structured light approach into an invisible structured light method if the projector signal and camera elements are adapted to work in the infrared range. This is the range of light the Kinect uses so the user doesn't actively see light coming from the device.

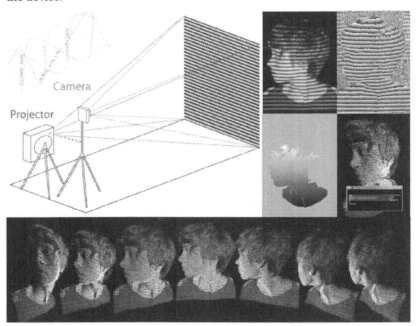

Figure 2-4. *Visible structured light setup pictured with a three–phase scanning technique. Lower frame shows resulting point cloud imagery that can be viewed from any angle.* Image licensed by Kyle MacDonald under Creative Commons Attribution 3.0 Unported.

Kinect's structured light approach is similar in principle to the technique used to scan visible light, as seen in Figure 2-4. A projector transmits a signal, a camera reads the signal, and computations are made to derive the distance of the objects from the camera for every pixel in the resulting depth image. However, the implementation details of Kinect's approach, as designed by PrimeSense, are unique. Instead of projecting a visible stream of changing shapes or bands of light, the invisible infrared laser projector generates a static cloud of variably intense dots in a pattern that appears to be random. An infrared laser striking a diffraction grating creates each of the dots by splitting the beam into thousands of individual points of light.

How many dots of infrared light does Kinect project onto a scene? Some estimate 30,000 to 300,000 dots. One curious person went through the trouble of documenting the pattern and reconstructing it on a grid in order to understand how the dots were structured. His conclusion was that a 3×3 grid is a repetition of a 211 x 165 spot pattern, which creates an overall grid of 633 x 495 or 313,335 points of light in total (see `http://azttm.wordpress.com/2011/04/03/kinect-pattern-uncovered/` for more information).

These dots look like random static, until you see that there is a repeating pattern with nine sections that make up a checkerboard. This light array is visible using a program like RGBDemo, which provides access to the IR image stream. The pattern is structured in a way that makes the detection of any set of dots registerable within the scope of the entire set – this is the essence of the architecture behind the PrimeSense depth sensor system (Figure 2-5). Because they are structured in such a recognizable way, the PrimeSense image processor chip can align these dots and make calculations based on them by comparing their different positions in order to create a reference image. When these cameras and chips are assembled into a system in the factory, all the components are calibrated by pointing the sensors at a wall, which are a specific distance from the device. The projector displays its structured pattern, and the IR camera captures an image that is stored on the PrimeSense chip as a registration of depth for all of the pixels in the image using that particular distance. For now on, this image becomes the reference point for calculating the distance to each pixel in a live depth image. The person's face disrupts the uniform pattern and is compared to the reference image in a process that derives the distance to each dot on the face within centimeters.

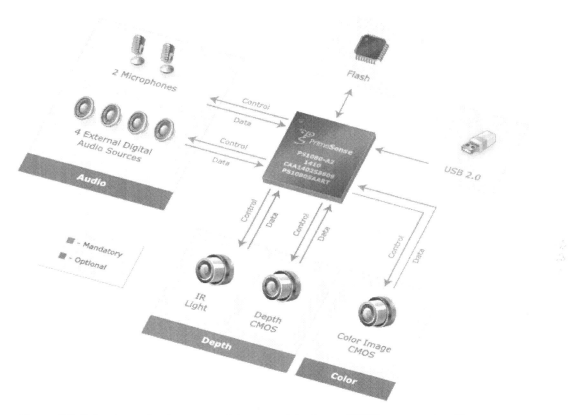

Figure 2-5. *PrimeSense depth sensor architecture. Color image CMOS sensor and audio components, colored blue, are not required to produce a depth map. Image courtesy of PrimeSense.*

A special camera that can see infrared light is required to read all of the dots. This is the camera behind Kinect's far right lens (Figure 1-6, D). This camera has a filter that masks the visible spectrum of light by only allowing infrared light to hit the light sensors behind it. If you look closely at this lens, you can see its iridescent green coating, which is how you can identify it from the visible light camera to its left. This barrier reflects all the unnecessary visible light that is not required for the depth calculating process, and only allows the infrared–projected dots to make it past the lens.

Kinect comes with another camera that is more familiar to us. It's a simple webcam, similar to what your laptop or phone might contain that captures visible light as red–green–blue, or RGB pixels. The PrimeSense reference devices have this camera as well. However, another licensee, Asus, chose not to include the RGB camera in their first WAVI Xtion unit. This camera is not used to generate the depth map, yet is included in many new depth camera units as a method of mixing visible light imagery and depth imagery together. Systems that combine visible light with depth maps are a form of volumetric camera, especially when they are assembled in an array of multiple RGB/depth–sensing devices. Combining an array of sensors can produce imagery without shadows where no depth information is stored, which allows for an infinite perspective on a scene without noticeable gaps behind the objects.

Additionally, visible light cameras can be used for computational analysis. For example, computer vision recognition software, such as OpenCV, can be applied to a scene to search for faces, and be trained to associate those faces with individual users who are isolated from the depth map. There are a variety of existing libraries and methods for deriving meaningful information from RGB imagery that can be integrated into an application when the hardware uses this additional visible light camera.

The following subsections describe a number of depth sensors that implement the structured light approach for deriving 3D scene information. They all utilize the PrimeSense design, but have different choices for optional internal components and form factors. As PrimeSense continues to license the design to more manufacturers, such as those producing flat screen TVs and set top boxes, developers will find an ecosystem of choices that can be applied to design applications based on what they know about Kinect. Many of these hardware manufacturers will choose to participate in OpenNI–compliant or other standards–based app stores, which creates opportunities for app developers to distribute their creations to a larger base of installed devices.

PrimeSense Reference Design

PrimeSense is an Israel–based company that makes the 3D–structured light technology that Microsoft licensed for use in Kinect. A reference design product is available for developers to evaluate the technology for use in new hardware, or for working with the OpenNI/NITE software that will be covered in subsequent chapters. For the scope of this book, PrimeSense's reference design is the same as Kinect's. The only differences are the lack of a motor, the need for an A/C power supply, and different microphone components. The PS1080 design (Figure 2-6) was the first available and is being replaced by a smaller model with a built-in stand. (More information is available at `http://www.primesense.com`).

▓ **Tip** The Xtion Pro Live manufactured by ASUS and mentioned in the next section is an exact implementation of the PrimeSense reference design. If you want an implementation of the reference design and have trouble getting the one from PrimeSense, the Xtion Pro Live is a good option.

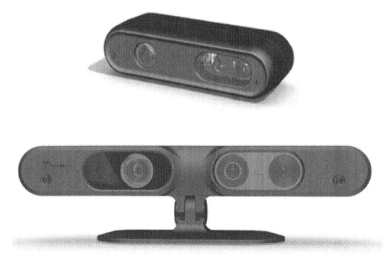

Figure 2-6. *The original PrimeSense reference design, the PS1080 (top), and the newer design (bottom)*

PrimeSense is the primary designer of infrared structured light systems. However, other hardware manufacturers produce depth imagery using alternative techniques that are described in upcoming section "Time–of–Flight Camera Systems". It is important to remember that regardless of the design, all of these sensors generate a depth map that can be incorporated into software using similar principles. As we get to the driver section of the stack, you'll see that there are layers of software that abstract out the particular hardware implementation and simply give you access to the 3D data regardless of the method used to generate it.

ASUS WAVI Xtion PRO and PRO Live

ASUS, a Taiwanese computer manufacturer, was the second major licensee of the PrimeSense hardware technology after Microsoft. The WAVI Xtion PRO is marketed as "the world's first and only professional PC motion–sensing software development kit." The distinction is warranted because, unlike Kinect, this product was designed with the intention of connecting it to a personal computer right out of the box and is developer–friendly with software and content creation tools intentionally included. Developers who build OpenNI–compliant software will have an opportunity to sell it in the ASUS Xtion store that will accompany the WAVI Xtion product line.

More recently, ASUS has introduced the Xtion PRO Live. This newer model includes an RGB camera, and is a precise implementation of PrimeSense's reference design. More information about both models is available at http://event.asus.com/wavi/Product/WAVI_Pro.aspx.

▓ **Note** Following is the direct link to the ASUS store page from which you can purchase the PRO Live model:

http://us.estore.asus.com/index.php?l=product_detail&p=4001.

Time–of–Flight Camera Systems

In contrast to structured light systems, time–of–flight camera systems don't make use of a complex projected pattern that needs to be decoded in order to calculate depth. Instead, these systems make use of the constant speed of light, approximately 300 million meters per second, as the key to unlocking the depth of objects in a scene. This depth ranging technique works by recording the time it takes a light signal to travel from an emitter and bounce off an object in a scene, and eventually land back on a light sensor in the unit. Extremely sensitive photo sensors and high–speed electronic components allow for a calculation of distance to be made based upon the time it takes for the light to travel and bounce back. This calculation is performed for every element in the sensor array, which requires the resolution of these devices to be smaller than that of structured light systems, usually between 64x48 and 320x240 pixels.

There are a number of techniques—such as pulsed light, RF modulation, and range gating—that manufacturers can use to make a time–of–flight system. Additionally, one can choose what type of light source to use, which determines the price and suitability of a given environment. An array of LEDs can be used to construct a consumer–priced system that works well for close range subjects, between two centimeters and two meters. Laser light–based systems have the ability to extend up to two kilometers, but these are out of the price range for anyone but large institutions.

LED–based time–of–flight sensors make up the bulk of the competition against PrimeSense structured light depth sensors. The following section highlights the devices that are marketed for use in 3D natural interface systems. Because of the way these systems are designed, they have abilities that structured light systems are unable to match. Depending on the type of illumination employed and the availability of ambient light suppression, time–of–flight units can be used outdoors in daylight. Structured light systems are often unable to compete with the strength of light beyond indoor conditions. Additionally, time–of–flight chip timing can be altered to provide depth precision over a large distance, or it can be densely tuned to a small depth range, making these systems suitable for facial capture where a high degree of detail is required over a short distance.

SoftKinetic DepthSense Cameras

SoftKinetic is a Belgium–based company that is bringing its DepthSense line of cameras to the US market along with their 3D gesture recognition middleware, iisu. Their DepthSense cameras gather 3D scene information using time–of–flight systems and include an RGB camera for sensing visible light imagery similar to Kinect. Their DepthSense hardware enables the natural motion based interface for the first game console designed for the Chinese market, iSec (`http://www.eedoo.cn/html/eedoo/isec/`). More information about SoftKinetic is available at `http://www.softkinetic.com/`.

PMD [vision] time–of–flight cameras

PMDTec, headquartered in Germany, is the world's leading supplier of integrated circuit technology for time–of–flight cameras. Their PMD[vision] CamBoard reference design has a grid of 200x200 sensor elements and provides companies that want to build their own products around this technology with an idea of how it can be implemented, similar to the relationship between PrimeSense and Microsoft with Kinect. The PMD [vision] O3 on the other hand, is packaged to be purchased direct from PMD and contains a sensor grid of 64x48 elements. These two devices (shown in Figure 2-7) do not come with an integrated RGB camera so they can only provide a depth and IR map. PMDTec's newest high–resolution prototypes capture up to 352x288 sensor elements. (More information is available at `http://www.pmdtec.com/`).

Figure 2-7. *The PMD [vision] CamCube, PMD [vision] CamBoard reference design, and PMD [vision] ConceptCam. Photo by Kara Dahlberg.*

Panasonic D-Imager

Panasonic's D-Imager shown in Figure 2-8 is marketed as a depth–sensing solution for gaming systems and digital signage. It was used to drive an interactive display at the Japanese pavilion during the World's Fair EXPO 2010 in Shanghai. The D-Imager can produce a 160x120-resolution depth map image at up to 30 frames per second. Panasonic's device contains back light suppression technology to make it more resilient to bright ambient light conditions. More information is available at `http://panasonic-electric-works.net/D-IMager`.

Figure 2-8. *Panasonic D-Imager time–of–flight depth sensor with an array of near infrared LEDs hidden to the left and right of the lens.*

Drivers & Data

Each of the devices mentioned in the previous hardware sections require drivers that can interpret the raw signals coming out of them and turn those signals into usable data for applications. Drivers are the next layer in the technology stack and are critical for developing software that can take full advantage of these devices on a given platform.

The original manufacturers only provide drivers for these devices on platforms that they support. This was the case with Kinect when it was initially released. Kinect was only usable on Xbox 360 systems until the open source community reverse–engineered the device to produce the OpenKinect project and the libfreenect drivers. Since then, there are multiple ways to work with Kinect on the platform you desire, or with any of the other depth–sensing cameras listed in the previous hardware section. This is all thanks to the magic of drivers – let's look at the kind of data supplied by different drivers.

OpenKinect/Libfreenect

The OpenKinect project's "libfreenect" open source driver for Kinect was the first available for general use and is the basis for a number of projects. Once the OpenNI driver framework came out, many projects dropped their dependencies on 'libfreenect' and moved over to the OpenNI drivers because they offered more flexibility for swapping out Kinect for other hardware, as well as a more robust set of features to build applications on top of. That said, many programmers still choose to use the "libfreenect" driver because it is easy to redistribute without requiring users to download dependent software.

Libfreenect provides access to three main sets of data from Kinect in the form of imagery. The most important data is the raw depth map image (Figure 2-9). This is libfreenect's only way of providing depth information for your application. This image is encoded to an 11-bit depth and the intensity values map to a specific distance from the camera. The rawest form of data displays this in shades of gray, yet most utilities choose to display it as a colored image in order to distinguish between distances visually.

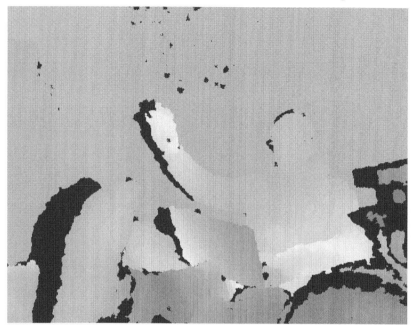

Figure 2-9. Depth map image from Libfreenect. Each color represents a distance from the camera.

The libfreenect driver also provides your application with a raw infrared (IR) image using the far right camera (Figure 2-10). The driver uses a direct feed from the camera that is designed to look for the dots of light produced by the IR projector. For that reason, image is filled with a speckled pattern that is dispersed around the objects in the scene. Because the IR map is used to generate the depth map, combining the two in a point cloud view provides a well–aligned 3D representation. However, the representation must be calibrated. This need for calibration is one of the frustrating aspects of using the Libfreenect drivers – OpenNI provides a calibrated mapping of the RGB data for the depth data.

Figure 2-10. *IR map image from Libfreenect. Speckled dots are projected on the scene from the IR projector.*

The final image data provided by Libfreenect is the visible light RGB image (Figure 2-11) from the middle camera in Kinect. The RGB camera provides the visual data you would work with to perform calculations on a scene using computer vision software, such as OpenCV, for face recognition. As you'll see in Chapter 3's coverage of the Body Dysmorphia Toy and the Ultra Seven/Kamehameha apps, this visual data can also be fed back into the software you produce to provide an augmented reality view. Your application can also align the RGB image data with the depth map to produce point clouds that will reconstruct a scene like 3D Capture-It, which is also covered in Chapter 3.

Figure 2-11. RGB map image from libfreenect

In addition to the image–based sensor data, Libfreenect also provides access to the 3-axis accelerometer chip embedded in Kinect. This could be helpful for designing hand-held applications that require users to move Kinect manually, as MatterPort does in Chapter 3. Libfreenect lets your application read data, but it also control actuators on Kinect. The LED light can turn different colors and turn on and off according to your design. The Kinect head can be tilted 30 degrees up or down using the motor–control function.

OpenNI

As described on www.OpenNI.org, "the OpenNI organization is an industry–led, not–for–profit organization formed to certify and promote the compatibility and interoperability of Natural Interaction (NI) devices, applications, and middleware." To carry out this mission, and with the strong support of PrimeSense, the organization has created an open source framework called OpenNI that provides an application–programming interface (API) for writing applications that use natural interaction. The API covers communication with low–level devices, such as vision and audio sensors, as well as high–level middleware solutions for visual tracking using computer vision.

OpenNI provides access to all of the data available through the Libfreenect driver. It also provides benefits such as methods for converting from projective x, y coordinates of the depth map back to real world x, y, and z coordinates in centimeters. This makes it easier to acquire a point cloud and generate alternate viewpoints in a scene from synthesized camera views (see Figure 2-12). Additionally this software provides the ability to track multiple people, and extract their gestures from skeletal body data.

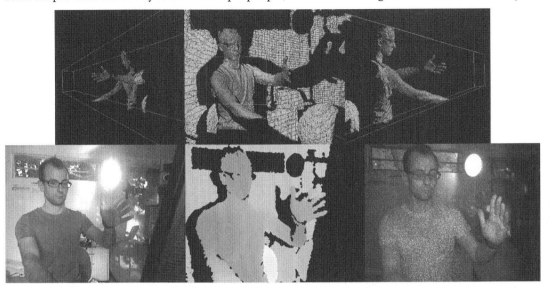

Figure 2-12. Upper row, point cloud rotated to show alternate viewpoints. Lower row, source RGB, depth, and IR map images for point cloud scene.

Commercial Drivers

The various software development kits designed to build applications for natural interaction all come with their own series of drivers for Kinect and have other depth sensors built in. SoftKinetic's issu, Omek Interactive's Beckon, and Gesturetek's GestTrack3D have their own implementations and may have varying ways of working with the device. In terms of the microphone array inside Kinect, Microsoft's drivers for Windows contain features not available in other drivers. Microsoft's Kinect SDK is not yet licensable for commercial use, but we expect that situation to change early in 2012 when Microsoft releases a commercial version of their SDK.

Middleware and Application Development Environments

The last major component of the stack is the so–called Middleware – various modules of software that act on sensor data and produce new functionality that an application can use. This type of functionality may be incorporated into integrated application development environments so the degree to which you are made aware of them as separate middleware modules depends on the software environment you are using to design your application.

The ability to segment the depth map into isolated users (Figure 2-13, left) that are separated from the background, or to extract and track a user's hand (Figure 2-13, right) are functional time–saving modules that can help you develop applications more quickly, and that dramatically reduce your codebase's size.

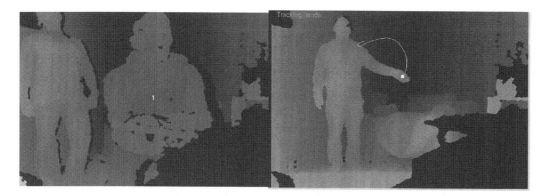

Figure 2-13. *Left, user segmentation tracking two people. Right, demonstration of a point tracking a hand*

The details of how to interface with this functionality may be different depending on the development environment you chose to work in. However, the underlying concepts are similar. Skeletal tracking middleware can track a user by segmenting that user into a skeleton with a series of "body data" joints. These joints can be assigned matching values in your application for puppeting a character or to listen for recognizable gestures.

As we move on to Chapter 3 and review applications in the wild, make note of how the programmers have used the methods we've identified in this chapter. Now that you're aware of how the technology works, you'll have a better idea of how to start making your own motion– and depth–aware apps.

CHAPTER 3

Applications in the Wild

In this chapter, we'll take a look at some applications built by developers in the PC Kinect app scene's first year that demonstrate the functionality you can take advantage of in your own programs. As you install the applications on your own computer, consider how the developers have leveraged the capabilities of the Kinect to create a unique experience in their applications. In later chapters, it will be your turn to design an application, so use this chapter for inspiration.

Control news and other realtime information from the Web with a wave of your hand using SenseCast. Practice your super powers as Ultra Seven or Kamehameha transforms your body movements into laser beams and exploding light. Freak yourself and your friends out as you adjust the "puffiness" of the world around you with the clever Body Dysmorphia Toy. Finally, discover the wonders of volumetric photography as an art form with MatterPort, an application that lets you scan the physical world to produce 3-D photographic models of objects and environments.

OTHER SOURCES FOR KINECT APPLICATIONS

When people first began sharing their experiments with the Kinect, replication on your own computer wasn't easy. Many developers posted videos of their work to YouTube that were picked up by sites such as KinectHacks.net and kinecthacks.com, These videos teased us all with the notion of what was possible.

OpenNI's Arena at http://arena.openni.org is a great place to look for inspiration and for programs to run on your computer. Currently, there are over 50 applications at the Arena. Zigfu.com takes the idea even further with a portal that lets you download its app store and then install and navigate new motion controlled apps that don't require you to touch a mouse or keyboard.

Sensecast: Minority Report Meets the Web

Sensecast is a program that was created to help designers and content creators easily wrap text, images, videos, RSS feeds, Twitter streams, and other Web-based media in a motion-controlled interface. Combined with an online service to manage the media you publish to your displays, Sensecast aims to be a complete authoring and publishing platform for motion-controlled content.

Sensecast is ideal for Web-like content such as photo slideshows and news feeds. The free Sensecast client software (which you download to your computer) pulls media from the Web and/or your local machine and arranges it in a series of menus and pages that you can then navigate with hand swipes and hovers. Just plug in your Kinect, download and launch the client, and voila! You're flicking text and images around the screen like it's 2054, as shown in Figure 3-1.

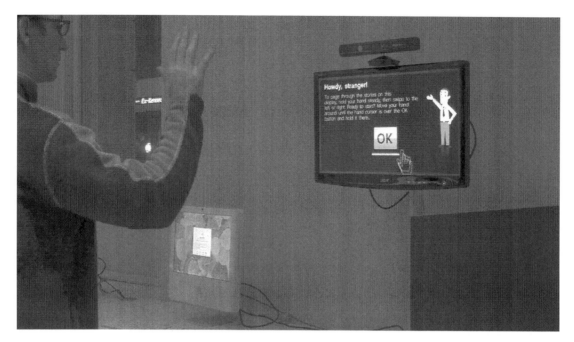

Figure 3-1. *Creator Jonathan C. Hall demos Sensecast's Kinect-aided motion controls.*

Created by one of our co-authors, Jonathan Hall, Sensecast aims to lower the barriers to entry for companies that want to put interesting content, rather than just signage and advertising, on public and quasi-public screens. We walk you through using the free client software in this chapter. However, Sensecast also offers a commercial version that integrates with social media channels, provides content performance metrics, etc. Of course, there's nothing to stop you from setting up Sensecast to run a Kinect-enabled display anywhere your heart desires, even in your own home. Want to flip through recipes for inspiration while kneading pizza dough in the kitchen? How about setting up a touch-free, germ-free bulletin and message board at your local school or community center? Or maybe you just want to build the coolest motion-controlled multimedia doorbell in your neighborhood. Sensecast can help.

In this exercise, we'll simply download and run the free client software available for Mac. More information is available online for those who want to tweak our Kinected display. Note that the Sensecast client can be configured to download assets from the Web or we can supply content manually for the display. Supplying your own content allows you to run Sensecast as a standalone without an Internet connection or content management system (CMS). The look and feel of the display is also completely customizable: you just have to edit the markup in the included presentation.xml file and add any of your own creative assets, such as fonts, images and sounds. In fact, there's a lot we can do with this little package. For those who want to explore beyond the simple content browser application presented in this section, there's an expanding library of tips and tricks available online.

Step 1: Download the Client

The first thing you'll want to do is find and download the latest build of the Sensecast client software for Mac by going to `http://sensecast.com/downloads`.

Download the Sensecast disk image file (.DMG) and double-click to mount if it does not mount automatically. You should see an install window something like the one in Figure 3-2.

Figure 3-2. *Sensecast installer window*

Step 2: Install the Dependencies

Next, you'll need to run the installer to set up the correct builds of Sensecast, OpenNI, NITE, and the device driver for your Kinect (or similar sensor). Double-click the installer, agree to the terms (if you want) and follow the instructions of the install process. The installer will ask you where you want to store Sensecast's data as shown in Figure 3-3. This is where all the program will look for settings and assets. By default, it creates a Sensecast folder in your Documents folder.

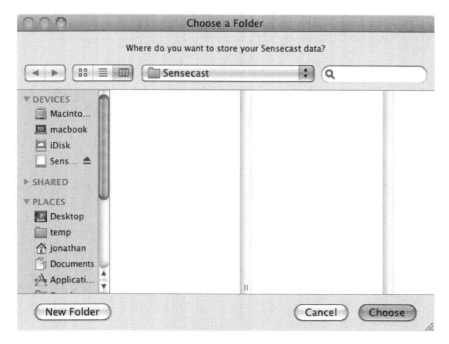

Figure 3-3. Sensecast installer dialog

In the final steps of the install process, you should probably reject the Advanced Option to run Sensecast on startup (which is intended for deployed Sensecast installations) and then select the sensor you want to setup, as shown in Figure 3-4.

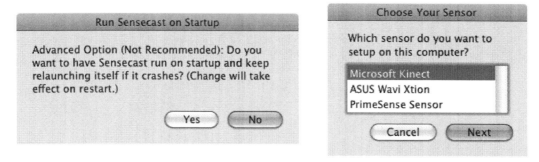

Figure 3-4. Sensecast installer dialog final steps

When the installer completes, go ahead and quit out of it. Now, as with the other Mac applications, Sensecast has placed an application icon in your Applications folder. Find it, plug in your Kinect and double click when ready!

Step 3: Launch Sensecast

Launch Sensecast to see how the application runs out of the box. A motion-controlled image and news browser will appear, as shown in Figure 3-5. Now, your whole screen is filled with Kinected-content joy!

Figure 3-5. *The Sensecast app that ships with the software*

Step 4: Rock Out!

By default, Sensecast uses only the hand-tracking machinery of OpenNI/NITE for navigation and requires a "focus gesture" before it will start tracking your hand. If you're standing in front of the display and you move around a little bit, you will be prompted to "Wave your hand back and forth to take control of the screen." Go ahead and wave at the screen until you see the hand cursor appear and the feedback image indicate that it's now tracking your hand. Now, as the Xbox folks say, you are the controller!

Take a minute to explore the Sensecast demo. Find the hover controls and the swipe controls by roaming the interface with the hand cursor. Browse the dummy content. This demo shows you the basic set of elements and interactions that you can use to make your own content similarly navigable by handwaving magic. If this kind of thing floats your boat, you can check out http://sensecast.org to learn how to customize Sensecast and to see more examples.

Ultra Seven

Do you sometimes dream of conquering the universe and beyond? Try out the Ultra Seven program designed for Windows that will transform you into an intergalactic warrior. Ultra Seven is a popular Japanese superhero from the 1960's show of the same name. He is a soldier from Nebula M-78, who becomes smitten with Earth while on a mission to map the Milky Way. Ultra Seven has several signature moves that lend themselves well for use with the Kinect's gestural recognition capabilities.

Kinect-Ultra is available for Windows PCs with fairly fast CPUs and fairly advanced GPUs. You must have at least OpenGL 2.0 and programmable shader capabilities in your graphics card. If your machine meets those requirements, you shouldn't have too much of a problem. If it doesn't, please skip past this application and the Kamehameha application. This app is at OpenNI Arena, which can be found at `http://bit.ly/ultraseven`.

The project's original page, where you can read more detailed instructions, updates, and watch example videos is at `http://code.google.com/p/kinect-ultra/`. Check that you have the versions of OpenNI, NITE, and SensorKinect that will work with this application as indicated in the documentation.

Once you have followed these instructions and have everything you need, plug in your Kinect, and connect the Kinect to your computer. Open the application. Make sure the sensor can see you clearly and you have enough space to move around freely. If you are having trouble, please consult the FAQ at `http://code.google.com/p/kinect-ultra/wiki/FAQ_en`.

Going into the calibration pose with your arms up around your head will signal the sensor to "clothe" you in the Ultra Seven costume. Figure 3-6 shows you how this transformation should look. Now your body should be clothed in red, with your "skeleton" visible and a mohawkish boomerang perched on top of your head. You are now ready to battle monsters, aliens, and your cat.

Figure 3-6. Calibration pose transforms you into Ultra Seven!

The crest alighting your crown is called the Eye Slugger. This fashionable head topper doubles as a removable weapon. By reaching your hands to the back of your head, then thrusting them forward, you can hurl this weapon in the direction you are facing. Don't worry; it'll return to you, too.

You can also place the Eye Slugger in midair. Stretch out your left arm to let the Kinect know what you're doing, then grab the weapon with your right hand, and place in front of you. Now you can move your forearm in a chopping motion to strike your opponent/cat/laundry hamper with the weapon, as shown in Figure 3-7.

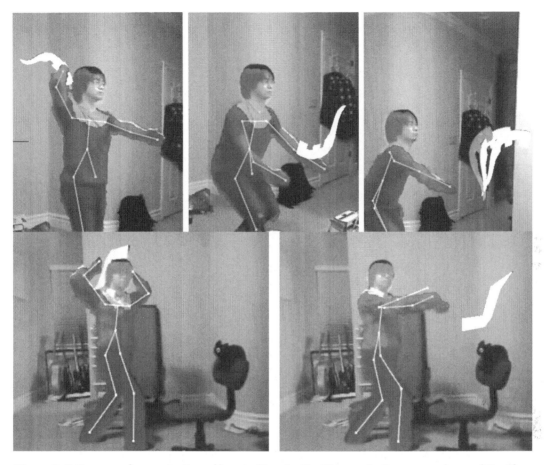

Figure 3-7. *Top row: demonstration of how to fling the Eye Slugger ; bottom row: advanced Eye Slugger maneuver*

Another trick up Ultra Seven's sleeve is the Wide Shot, which allows you to shoot out a super stream of energy by making an L shape with both arms. Bend your left arm across your chest and hold your right arm vertical from the elbow with your hand up. The energy stream will fire out in the direction that your body is oriented. Objects that the Kinect senses in the foreground will not be hit by the energy stream; instead, it will pass by such objects and continue on its path.

Lastly, you also have at your fingertips the Emperium Beam. In the TV show, this energy ray would shoot out from a green gem on Ultra Seven's forehead. Bring your fingers to the sides of your forehead to signal the beam. Aim! Fire! Figure 3-8 shows these slick moves.

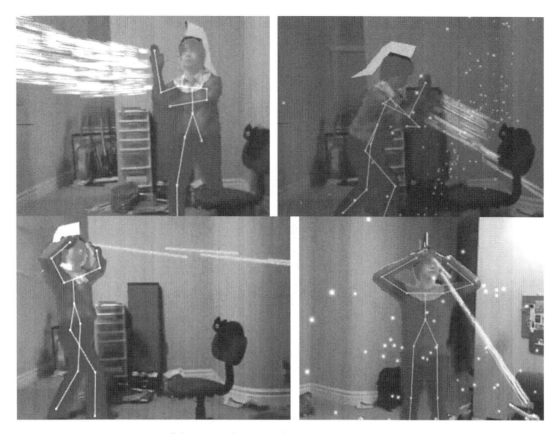

Figure 3-8. *Top row: a powerful stream of energy triggered with pose ; bottom row: Emperium Beam in action*

After a couple minutes of play, your superhero cloak will start to blink on and off, signaling that it is time for Ultra Seven to depart from Earth. In the TV show, the Ultramen could only stay on Earth for short periods of time. When you begin to flash, crouch down and then thrust upwards. Your avatar will shoot straight out the top of the screen, presumably bound for Nebula M-78 once again.

Kamehameha

A similar application by the same developer, Tomoto Washio, allows you to morph into a Super Saiyan. If you are not familiar with the Dragon Ball Z series, a Super Saiyan is a powerful, rage-induced transformation that may be achieved by advanced members of the Saiyan race under extraordinary circumstances. The result of the transformation is apparently a flaming, golden aura and hair that defies gravity, as shown in Figure 3-9.

This application is also available at OpenNI Arena. The short link to the site is `http://bit.ly/arkamehameha`, and additional information can be found on the project page at `http://code.google.com/p/kinect-kamehameha`. Like the previous superhero app, Kamehameha works on faster Windows PC computers only. Follow the instructions and suggestions on the site. Make sure you have the correct versions of OpenNI, NITE, and SensorKinect. Once you are ready, plug in your Kinect, connect the Kinect to your computer, and then open the application.

Standing in front of the Kinect sensor so that your body is visible, assume the standard calibration pose with arms up around your head and your elbows bent, as shown in Figure 3-9. Allow the sensor time to find your shape. You should begin to flash, and soon an aura and a head of electric hair will appear around you. If the sensor is having a hard time finding you, try switching to party mode for easier calibration.

Figure 3-9. *Kamehameha calibration and transformation*

Kamehameha was the name of the first king of Hawaii. He was purportedly born around 1738 when Haley's Comet was making its fiery journey across the sky. The timing was significant because legend at the time spoke of a great king born under a comet who would unify the islands.

In the Dragon Ball series, Kamehameha refers to a signature energy attack, which is the move that you will be able to perform with this application. The Kamehameha is formed when cupped hands are drawn in front of the user and their latent energy is concentrated into a single point between the cupped hands. The hands are then thrust forward to shoot out a streaming, powerful beam of energy. First, hold your hands close together so that the sensor can see them. You will see a white ball of light form between your hands that should look similar to the first image in the series in Figure 3-10.

Figure 3-10. *Kamehameha attack*

Keeping your hands cupped, bend from the knee to lower your center of gravity. This movement should signal the light to increase in intensity. From here, you can push the energy ball out from your hands in any direction. Extend your arms out in a controlled motion and hold them towards your target to see what happens.

If the motion detection isn't working very well, try switching to Party Mode. Please note that this technology is all relatively new, what some might call the bleeding edge, so developers are still trying to work the kinks out. Kamehameha isn't a title put out by a major game studio for sale on Xbox and understandably is not yet as polished as a commercial program. Tomoto's two Kinect apps are noteworthy for being a couple of the first apps out that really put the motion control abilities to use. Also, Tomoto provides all the code under an open source license for people to modify and learn from.

Body Dysmorphia

This Mac only app made with the Cinder creative coding framework is simple, but quite entertaining. Basically you can make yourself look fat or thin in realtime. Body dysmorphia is a psychological disorder that affects perhaps 1% of the population and causes the afflicted to obsess over a perceived defect in one's own appearance. Use this program created by Robert Hodgin to see yourself, your cat, and the world in Stay Puft Marshmellow form.

A quick link to the download the program is at `http://bit.ly/dysmorphia`, and you can learn more about the creator at `http://roberthodgin.com/` and `http://www.flight404.com/`. Take a look at the instructions on the first site and click the link to download the application. Keep in mind that this application will only work on a Mac operating system. Before opening the application, make sure that your Kinect is plugged in and also connected to your computer. Once the green light is visible , you can launch the application and start playing!

As soon as you open the program, you will see objects within the scope of your Kinect dysmorphed in realtime. At the bottom left-hand side of the screen, you will find a key for various adjustments to the image. Hold down the "P" key to inflate your subject and lowercase "p" to shrink it. Basically, the data from the Kinect is manipulated by increasing or decreasing the radius of the points in the cloud. This has a comical and cartoonish effect as you expand the points into puffy lumps and blobs. Do not expect a realistic-looking image, but instead have fun adjusting the colors and textures in various ways using the key.

Pressing "b" or "B" will adjust the amount of blur applied to the image. Adding blur by pressing down an uppercase "B" will smooth out the points along the surface so the image is less lumpy. Play around with the blur levels to find an amount you like in correlation to an amount of puffiness. If you turn the blur up all the way, the image will look extremely impressionistic and lose detail, especially if you also turn up the amount of puffiness, as shown in Figure 3-11. Increasing both blur and puffiness can also erase the appearance of depth.

Figure 3-11. *Body Dysmorphia Toy showing the user fully puffed and blurred*

Remember that the Kinect has a limited usable range of about 2' to 20'. Therefore, if you get too close or far away from the sensor, the dysmorphia filter will not work. The ideal range for using this application is around 5' to 10'.

Next to the key along the bottom edge of your screen, you will find the gray scale depth map that the infrared sensor has produced. Anything outside the recordable range of the Kinect will appear in black, as shown in Figure 3-12. You can use this guide and know that anything appearing in black will be clipped and unaffected by the dysmorphia filter.

Figure 3-12. *The Body Dysmorphia Toy applies puffiness to the user on the left within the range of depth sensor, but not to the user on the right who is too close to the sensor.*

You can also control what is viewable on your screen by adjusting the clipping plane. You can make adjustments to decrease the usable depth as an easy way to isolate your subject from an object-filled background. Simply adjust the clipping plane to include only the subject you are interested in, cutting out elements from the foreground or background you'd like to discard, as shown in Figure 3-13.

Figure 3-13. Body dysmorphia application used to clip information from the background

Hodgin's body dysmorphia app shows how a novel, yet very straightforward use of the camera and depth map data stream can provide an entertaining experience without even using gesture recognizers and body data mappings. The next app we will show will reveal another level of usage for the same data when matched with more sophisticated algorithms for 3-D scene reconstruction.

MatterPort

Photography takes a step towards its volumetric 3-D future with the software MatterPort. Go to `http://matterport.com` to download the application, which is currently available only for Windows. This program will allow you to easily take volumetric snapshots of objects or entire scenes and then stitch them together to be viewable from all angles in a single 3-D model.

Snapshots are automatically taken based on your movements. The idea is that you move around the room carrying the Kinect device. Every time you move to a new position and then pause, a picture is automatically taken. The software in combination with the Kinect is able to detect your motion and pausing, and take photos at each pause. You are thus able to capture an entire scene without returning to the keyboard over and over again.

After each photo, the system shows a rough alignment of the overall scene. You are then able to fill in the spots you missed. Once the basic alignments have been found, the program will spend some time optimizing the alignments for maximum visual quality.

Begin by plugging in your Kinect, connecting the Kinect to your computer, and opening the MatterPort software. On the right hand side of the screen, you will see the MatterPort Controls, as shown in Figure 3-14. The top image on the screen will show the live camera view, which is what the Kinect is pointed at right at that moment. The image underneath will be the last good capture, which will update to show the past capture point as soon as you begin to capture a different image. You will use the control buttons at the bottom of the panel on the screen as you go through the process of capturing a scene. START is a toggle button that will initiate the capture and that you can use to pause and resume the process. Backup will let you go back and remove the last capture in the series. Restart lets you start all over again from scratch. The control buttons to the right enable you to refine a model, save a model, and load files.

Figure 3-14. MatterPort live camera view, last good capture, and the various control buttons

To capture the room you are in, stand in the middle of the room and point the Kinect at a corner. Click START, and MatterPort will begin to capture an image, as shown in Figure 3-15. You can click START, which serves as a PAUSE button once the capture begins, if you need to take a break from the process.

Figure 3-15. *MatterPort Cloud Viewer window to the left of the control panel showing start of process with one good capture displayed*

When the image is captured, the application will make a sound. Once you hear the sound, a screenshot will appear in the Last good capture section of the control panel. This screen will show the last scan taken. There is no need to check the screen as you continue to scan. Every time you hear the capture noise, you can quickly move the Kinect to a new position to cover more area in the room. The new position should overlap with at least some of the area from the previous capture. As more images are captured, they will automatically be aligned in the composite image.

Figure 3-16 shows how the 3D model gets built as you take more photos. The full-resolution of the most recent capture will appear in the Cloud Viewer window to the left of the MatterPort controls. The rest of the model will appear in reduced resolution. You can see in Figure 3-16 how the sharpest part of the image in the Cloud Viewer corresponds to the last good capture image in the control panel to the right.

Figure 3-16. *MatterPort capture in progress showing last good capture aligning with incoming capture information*

If you move the Kinect too fast, the alignment will fail. In such instances, move the camera so that the view is similar to that shown in the last good capture. If the program does not create proper alignment between items, you can repeatedly hit Backup to go back until the bad alignment is removed. After a large number of capture screens, objects may align only roughly, as shown in Figure 3-17.

Figure 3-17. *MatterPort showing a roughly aligned 3-D capture*

Use the mouse to browse around the composite image from different angles. Small misalignments are okay since they can be fixed by clicking Refine, which will create a final result like that shown in Figure 3-18. However, a large misalignment must generally be fixed by clicking Backup until the alignment problem is removed. This final screenshot will continue to show a reduced-resolution cloud, but a final full-resolution point cloud will be written to disk. Don't forget to save your final, composite image! MatterPort saves your composite image as a point cloud in a .ply file that can be opened in Meshlab, which you can find at `http://meshlab.sourceforge.net/`.

Figure 3-18. *MatterPort showing rough mesh enhanced by using the Refine button*

Now that you've walked through a number of different applications created by other users, start thinking about how you can approach designing your own. In the following chapters, you'll get acquainted with various development environments and see what it's like to put your ideas into action.

CHAPTER 4

Scripting the Kinect

Now that you've seen a little bit of what the Kinect can do, it's time to make it do your bidding! In this chapter, we will use the cross-platform, noob-friendly Processing programming environment—along with some Kinect libraries written by geniuses—to grab in–depth information from a Kinect sensor and do our own rendering and analysis of it. Sound amazing? Prepare to amaze yourself.

Processing

First, a response to those of you who are saying to yourselves, "Uh, why Processing?" (or perhaps more likely, "Uh, what's Processing?"). Processing is a sweet, little, self-contained programming language and integrated development environment (IDE) that came out of the famed MIT Media Lab in 2001. It was created by Ben Fry and Casey Reas, then two students in John Maeda's research group.

Originally, Processing was conceived as a software sketchbook for visual artists that would make it simple to do basic computer programming for visual applications. Today, Processing is a free and open source software platform for all kinds of interactive applications. It has scores of user-contributed libraries and is actively maintained, improved, and used by tens of thousands of artists, developers, hobbyists, and students.

What Processing Can Do For You

Processing is essentially a Java application and therefore can do everything that Java can do: drawing and animating 2D and 3D graphics; manipulating images, sound and video; reading and writing data; communicating via HTTP; and, of course, working with data from a Kinect sensor. But Processing has a scripting syntax and simplified function calls that make it easy for newcomers and efficient for pro coders of a certain stripe. It is "self-contained" in that it runs its own instance of the Java Virtual Machine (JVM) on your computer, so it's a cinch to set up: just download and launch. Like Java, Processing works across Windows, Mac, and Linux operating systems.

So, again, why Processing? If this is your first trip down the rabbit hole of computer programming, well, Processing is as easy as it gets. It is the gateway drug to hackerdom. But, even if you're a C++ heavyweight who writes your own Assembler hacks, Processing still has its charms: the "sketchbook" metaphor and pluggable libraries are a handy way to jump into exploring something completely new, like a new piece of 3D-seeing hardware!

Download, Install, Explore

If you're familiar with other IDEs, such as Visual Studio, Xcode, Eclipse, or even Adobe products like DreamWeaver, this is going to be the easiest setup of a programming environment you've ever experienced! If this is your first IDE, well, suck it up. It doesn't get any easier. In this section, we're going to download and install Processing, run some quick test code to make sure everything works, and then explore the setup of the IDE, the filesystem, and some of the included sample sketches so you get a sense of what Processing can do, and what you can do with Processing plus Kinect.

To download Processing, browse to `http://processing.org/download`, where you'll find download packages for each of the major operating systems (Windows, Mac OS X, and Linux) and a second Windows download for those of you who want to set up and use your own JVM separate from the included one (not recommended). Click the download link appropriate for you.

Unlike many pieces of software you may have installed before, there's no separate installer program with Processing. After you download it, you simply need to uncompress any compressed files, move them to wherever you keep applications on your computer (usually `C:\Program Files\Processing\` on Windows, `/Applications/Processing/` on Mac OS X, or `~/Applications/` on Linux), and launch the program. You're done! Well, almost.

It's a good idea to try building some super simple script to make sure everything's in working order, so let's do that. When you launch Processing, you'll see a blank code window, like that in Figure 4-1, open to a new "sketch." Let's run our first script to make sure we're set up correctly. Write these five lines of code into the code window, as shown in Figure 4-1, and click Run. The Run button is the circular "play" button at the top left corner of the application window. You should see results like those in Figure 4-2.

```
size(800, 600);
fill(255, 0, 0);
rect(10, 10, 10, 10);
text("Hello World", 25, 20);
print("It works!");
```

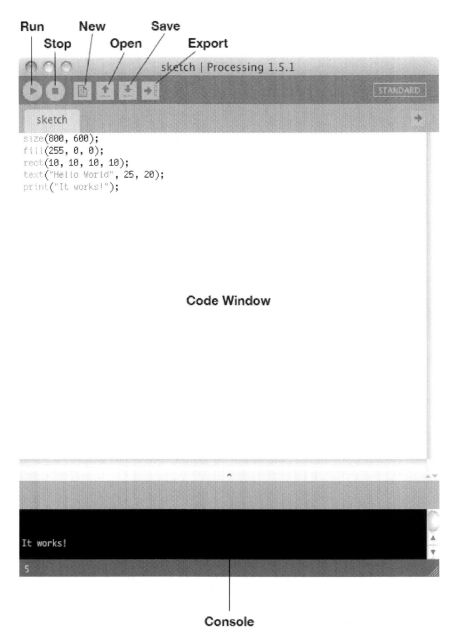

Figure 4-1. *Processing's application window*

Figure 4-2. *The output of our "Hello World" example*

Our little example script generated a new application window that's 800 pixels wide by 600 pixels tall. It then drew a 10-pixel-by-10-pixel red rectangle in the window starting at (10, 10) in (x, y) coordinate space and rendered the text "Hello World" next to that rectangle. Finally, our script printed a success message to the console. Got it? Good. Let's go just a tad deeper in preparation for using Processing to control the Kinect.

Processing Libraries and Sketches

Since we're going to spend some time with Processing in this chapter writing scripts and adding Kinect libraries written by third parties, you will not regret taking a little time now to browse the dozens of useful libraries and example sketches included with the main Processing distribution. These examples will give you an idea of how Processing works and what its capabilities are, as well as how the larger Processing user community has extended those capabilities to create a formidable free software platform for programming interactivity.

Included Examples

Start by taking a gander at the extensive list that opens under `File   Examples...` It should look something like the list shown in Figure 4-3. Open one of the sketches under "Topics" that seems interesting to you.

Want to render cool visual effects? Check out the Firecube example under "Effects." Looking to build your own graphical user interface (GUI)? See how simple button and scrollbar elements are implemented under the "GUI" topic. How about eerily complex and cool physics? Try a bunch of the "Motion" examples.

Figure 4-3. *The "palette" of examples in Processing*

Once you've seen enough to convince you that Processing is worth your while, let's take a last peek under the hood before connecting the Kinect. Specifically, let's look at Processing's file organization and how to extend the functionality of the application ourselves using freely available code libraries on the Web.

Adding Libraries

A nice-but-not-comprehensive index of Processing libraries lives at `http://www.processing.org/reference/libraries/.` There are some great libraries for helping your Processing code interface with hardware, do advanced 3D work, and tie into other massively useful non-Processing code bases such as OpenCV, the open source computer vision library. If you use Processing again, you'll no doubt want to know how to add some of this free contributed code.

When you first launched Processing, a new sketch was created with the naming convention `sketch_datex`. If you're following along, you created a 5-line "Hello World" script. Now, let's save that sketch to our "Sketchbook." Go ahead and click **Save**. Processing creates a sketchbook folder inside your operating system's main documents folder, something like `C:\My Documents\Processing\` on `Windows` and `/Documents/Processing` on Mac OS X, depending on how your system is set up. In Processing's "Preferences" pane, you can see—and change—the location of the sketchbook on the filesystem. In any case, find out where it is and browse to that location.

Your Processing sketchbook is just a folder that contains any sketches or libraries you've created or added from third parties. You should now see a folder inside it called `sketch_datex`, or whatever you named your sketch if you gave it a name. Every Processing sketch gets its own folder, which helps keep all related files and assets together.

Since you haven't yet added any contributed libraries to Processing, you won't have a "libraries" folder in your sketchbook folder. Let's fix that now. Create a folder inside your sketchbook folder called "libraries." Note that you must name this folder "libraries," as that is the specific name that Processing looks for. In the next section, you will drop downloaded Kinect library files into it, relaunch Processing, and voila! The libraries will be installed. Every time Processing starts up, it searches the sketchbook folder for stuff to load. Sketches are arranged in the fly-out menus under File Sketchbook. Contributed libraries are arranged under Sketch>Import Library…>Contributed. Whenever you add files to the sketchbook and libraries folders like this, you have to relaunch Processing for the new libraries to become available to your sketches and show up in the menu. Without further ado, let's add Kinect libraries and start scripting the Kinect!

Finally Kinecting

Unfortunately, here is where PC, Mac, and Linux users must part ways. As of this writing, there's no single Kinect library for Processing that does it all on all platforms. But that will change (if it hasn't already by the time you read this)! Processing is constantly being extended by a devoted community of hackers, and there's a particularly active group dedicated to unleashing the power of Kinect and Kinect-like sensors. Once you feel comfortable with how this works, you might even take a look around `http://www.processing.org/reference/libraries/` for Kinect projects other than the ones we use below.

We use two Kinect-for-Processing libraries here: dLibs for Windows by Thomas Diewald and openkinect for Mac by Daniel Shiffman. Both of these projects implement partial functionality of the Kinect using the drivers and libraries that are part of the open source libfreenect project, the pinnacle accomplishment (so far!) of the OpenKinect community at `http://openkinect.org` and mentioned in the Introduction. Although much of this book covers codebases that originated in commercial enterprises and are partly or completely proprietary, this chapter is built entirely on free and open source software

(FOSS) shared by talented hackers all over the world. Before jumping into the Windows-, Mac-, and Linux-specific directions to follow, bask in the glow of that!

Kinect for Processing on Windows

Now that we've installed Processing, getting Kinect to work with it on your PC is a simple matter of installing some compatible drivers and running some example code. For this, we turn to Thomas Diewald's dLibs project.

Adding dLibs

Let's do this. Browse to the dLibs code repository on GitHub: `https://github.com/diwi/dLibs`. Click "Downloads" and select the `.zip` package to download somewhere on your computer. Unzip the folder and inside you'll see a `README` document and a folder called "dLibs_freenect." Copy or move the whole "dLibs_freenect" folder into your newly-minted "libraries" folder inside Processing's sketchbook folder. Now, do the exact same thing with Jonathan Feinberg's PeasyCam library, which dLibs uses in some of its included examples. Download the zip archive from `http://mrfeinberg.com/peasycam/#download` and move "peasycam" into your "libraries" folder. Whew! That's a lot of folder shuffling, but that's it! Relaunch Processing and you should see `dLibs_freenect` and `peasycam` now available to you under Sketch   Import Library...   Contributed.

Updating Drivers

We can't use the library until we've updated our Kinect drivers to the libfreenect ones it expects. If you already installed some Kinect drivers for Windows (e.g., to run `RGBDemo` in Chapter 1), we're going to update them here to use libfreenect. Fortunately, they come precompiled and included with the dLibs download. Unfortunately, you will probably also need to install the free, 5MB Microsoft Visual C++ 2010 Redistributable Package, which provides the runtime components necessary to use software compiled with Visual C++ 2010, which these libfreenect files were (please note that you do not need this package if you already have Visual C++ 2010 installed). Grab it at `http://www.microsoft.com/download/en/details.aspx?id=5555` or search "Microsoft Visual C++ 2010 Redistributable Package" if the link has changed. Download the package and run the installer.

   Now, make sure the Kinect is plugged into the PC with the power cord connected to the wall socket. When the hardware is connected, Windows will launch a wizard to install drivers for the three components—XBox NUI Motor, XBox NUI Audio, and XBox NUI Camera—or if you already installed some drivers or otherwise, put the kibosh on the search. You can launch the wizard yourself from the Device Manager (Control Panel   System   Device Manager). Find the three "XBox" components, probably under "Human Interface Components" (if already installed) or with big yellow question marks on them under "Other" (if not installed). If you have previously installed other Kinect drivers either with OpenNI or the Microsoft Kinect SDK, you may see these devices set up under different headings in the Device Manager. Right-click on each of the components and select "Update Driver Software..." As of this writing, Windows will not find drivers for the Kinect using Windows Update, and you don't want it to. Instead, steer the driver installation wizard to the `kinect_driver_windows` folder inside `dLibs_freenect/library`. Once all three drivers are added, we're ready to launch one of the dLibs samples.

Running the Pointcloud Example

In Processing, under Processing   Examples..., you should now see some additional examples under the contributed libraries. For comparison with RGBDemo from Chapter 1, let's look first at the dLibs "pointcloud" example: kinect_basic_3d_pointcloud

Open and run the example. Right out of the box, the output of the sketch should look like Figure 4-4. If you click and drag inside the window or use your mouse scroll wheel, you can alter the "camera" perspective on the image/depth data (thanks to PeasyCam!) to something like that shown in Figure 4-5. You'll notice that the output of this sketch is a lot like that of RGBDemo in Chapter 1, only now you can see the script and edit it right in Processing!

Figure 4-4. *The dLibs pointcloud sketch, run as is*

Figure 4-5. *The dLibs pointcloud sketch with the perspective changed by clicking and dragging inside the window*

What the Pointcloud Sketch is Doing

A typical, very basic Processing sketch consists of a `setup()` function—called at the outset to set up any parameters or processes used by the sketch—and a `draw()` function, which runs on the main loop, constantly drawing and redrawing any elements you tell it to, whether static or animated. The pointcloud sketch follows that convention with a few additional things going on: some preliminary library import statements and variable declarations, an initialization routine for PeasyCam, which is used to control the virtual "camera", or perspective on the rendered 3D scene, and `drawPointcloud()`, a custom-defined function that grabs all the points in the Kinect3D object and draw them. There is also a `stop()` function that gets called whenever the sketch is terminated.

It's almost always instructive to look at the code and try to understand what it's doing. Here, for example, is the original code for the `drawPointcloud` function and some of the variables used by it:

```
Kinect3D k3d_;

int kinectFrame_size_x = VIDEO_FORMAT._RGB_.getWidth();
int kinectFrame_size_y = VIDEO_FORMAT._RGB_.getHeight();

void drawPointcloud(){

  KinectPoint3D kinect_3d[] = k3d_.get3D();

  int jump = 5;

  int cam_w_ = kinectFrame_size_x;
  int cam_h_ = kinectFrame_size_y;

  strokeWeight(3);

  for(int y = 0; y < cam_h_-jump ; y+=jump){
    for(int x = 0; x< cam_w_-jump*2 ; x+=jump){
      int index1 = y*cam_w_+x;

      if (kinect_3d[index1].getColor() == 0 )
        continue;

      stroke(kinect_3d[index1].getColor() );

      float cx = kinect_3d[index1].x;
      float cy = kinect_3d[index1].y;
      float cz = kinect_3d[index1].z;
      point(cx, cy, cz);

    }
  }
}
```

I know what you're saying to yourself: Kinect3D object? What and where is that? And what about KinectPoint3D inside the **drawPointcloud()** function? Where did that come from, and how do I know what it does? Here it's instructive to look through the documentation included with dLibs, which at least identifies the properties and methods associated with all of the objects available from the library. Open the included **dLibs_freenect/reference/index.html** in your browser.

Although the documentation is bare bones, you can see that the Kinect3D object manages data collection from the Kinect, including frame rate, calibration, depth, and RGB images, etc. Calling the function **get3D()** on the Kinect3D object like the example does inside **drawPointcloud()** returns a 640×480 array of points or pixels, each of which has both color (RGB) and position (X, Y, Z`) values, sometimes called RGBZ data because it merges traditional RGB camera data (a 2D color image) with depth information (the position of each pixel of that image on the Z axis). The library object for holding each point is a KinectPoint3D object and so the sketch creates an array of these objects each time it calls **drawPointcloud()** and stores it there.

```
KinectPoint3D kinect_3d[] = k3d_.get3D();
```

Tweaking the Example

After you've played around with the example as is, let's try modifying it a bit. Specifically, let's tweak the `drawPointcloud()` function and see what happens.

Higher Resolution

The first thing you can try is changing up the resolution of the rendered image. You can see that the integer variable jump is used to skip over points in each array of RGBZ values coming from our Kinect3D object. Try changing

```
int jump = 5;
```

to

```
int jump = 1;
```

Rendering every single data point rather than every fifth data point will take its toll on the program's execution, which you'll notice in the slower frame rate when you run the sketch this time. Still, you should also notice quite a bit more detail in the rendered image like those in Figures 4-6 and 4-7.

Figure 4-6. Our hi-res pointcloud reveals a new detail in the scene: a cat!

Figure 4-7. *The hi-res pointcloud, tilted*

Depthmap

Alternatively, you might want your rendered image to show a different type of information, not just the visible light RGB data. You might, for example, want the depth information somehow encoded in the color of each pixel in the rendering, creating what's called a "depthmap." This example uses Processing's `stroke()` function to render the pointcloud, where the color argument for the stroke is taken from the KinectPoint3D. Now, let's take this value from the depth value at that pixel instead.

```
Replacestroke(kinect_3d[index1].getColor() );
```

    with

```
float depth = (10 +kinect_3d[index1].z)/10;
stroke(color(255* depth, 255* depth, 255* depth));
```

    Essentially, we're replacing the RGB color of the image with a gray value based on the distance of the point from the Kinect. Now, objects that appear closer to the Kinect should be brighter than objects farther away. We should note here that the Z values in our KinectPoint3D object are in negative meters (distance in front of the camera) and are floating-point (decimal) numbers. So, if the tip of my nose is exactly a meter and a third away from the connect, the Z value will be something like -1.333333, and the transformation we've applied above to get the color will be affected accordingly. If you run the sketch, you should see something like Figure 4-8.

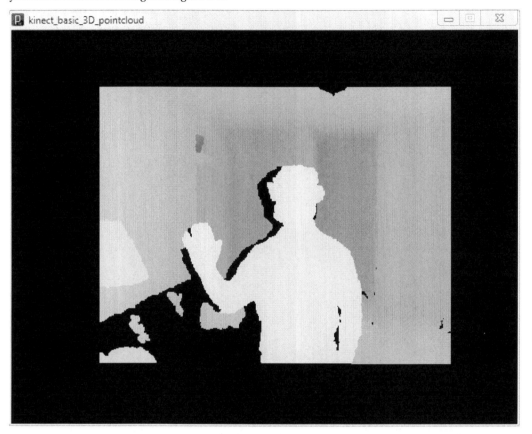

Figure 4-8. *The pointcloud sketch turned into a depthmap*

Thresholding

That's all fine and good, but not incredibly useful. What really unlocks the power of the Kinect is the ability to selectively analyze the 3D space in front of the sensor, to pick out objects and people in the scene, and understand what's happening with them. What is the object? Is the person holding the object? Is the person gesturing? Such questions form a classic topic in machine vision known as scene analysis that has been extensively developed using 2D images over the past few decades. With the added depth information from a Kinect-like sensor or depth camera, scene analysis becomes much easier and more robust and the possibilities grow.

We can already begin to see these possibilities by modifying this sketch ever so slightly. We've altered the rendering so that its colors reflect depth, but now let's try selecting only pixels from the Kinect within a certain depth range, a technique called thresholding. Note these two lines in the example code:

```
if (kinect_3d[index1].getColor() == 0 )
     continue;
```

As `drawPointcloud()` is looping through the 640×480 array of points, these lines tell the draw function to just drop any black points typically associated with object "shadows." In the following example, an additional directive to drop any points beyond a depth of 2 meters has been added:

```
if (kinect_3d[index1].z < -2)
     continue;
```

Finally, we can comment out the earlier edits we made to create the depthmap with the "//" comment characters. Now when we run the sketch, points must meet a certain depth threshold in order to be rendered at all. In this case, anything more than 2 meters from the Kinect will be dropped, most of it is probably background stuff. If you're just a meter or two away from your Kinect and it's clear behind you when you run this sketch, you should see yourself fairly cleanly cut out from the black void behind you as in Figure 4-9.

Figure 4-9. Thresholding example, with a poorly calibrated Kinect

When you have a camera that sees in 3D, it's that easy to pick out a very well-defined region of interest in 3D space for further analysis. Now that you have your likeness as a cutout, what do you want to do with it? We'll explore more in later chapters.

Kinect for Processing on Mac OS X

Getting Processing to talk to the Kinect on Mac OS X is a bit easier than on Windows, thanks to ITP's Daniel Shiffman, who released his library based on libfreenect within weeks of the Kinect's release.

Adding OpenKinect

To install Shiffman's library, simply browse to `http://www.shiffman.net/p5/kinect/` and download the `openkinect.zip` file, which contains the compiled library and some sketch examples. You'll be able to dig a bit deeper into the examples if you also take a look at the source on GitHub: `https://github.com/shiffman/libfreenect/tree/master/wrappers/java/processing`. Put this whole folder inside your "libraries" folder inside your Processing sketchbook folder and, as always, relaunch Processing.

Updating Drivers

Unlike on Windows, here we're able to let Processing drive the hardware directly—there's no separate process to set up the Kinect or install drivers. You're ready to go!

Running the Pointcloud Example

Let's launch the included pointcloud example code as a point of reference. Under Examples... Contributed Libraries openkinect, you should see three or so examples. Open Pointcloud and click Run. You should see something like Figure 4-10, yet another pointcloud not unlike that of the RGBDemo program.

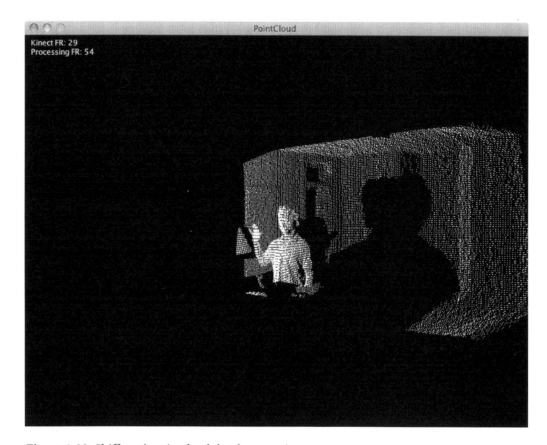

Figure 4-10:.*Shiffman's pointcloud sketch, run as is*

What the Pointcloud Sketch is Doing

Again, we have an output that's a bit like `RGBDemo` from Chapter 1, only we can play with it in Processing! This sketch obeys the convention in Processing of having a `setup()` function to set up any parameters or processes used by the sketch and a `draw()` function that repeats as the sketch runs, drawing and redrawing elements. As with the Windows examples, there's some other stuff going on too: import statements to import the necessary library elements, some variable declarations, some helper functions to get the data from the `Kinect()` object into the form the sketch needs to produce the rendering, and, of course, a `stop()` function that gets called when the sketch is terminated.

Speaking of the `Kinect()` object, uh, what is it? If you read through the Windows example, you learned that dLibs breaks up the data from the Kinect into a few different classes, and there was some basic documentation for them included with the library. The openkinect library also wraps the Kinect data with a few classes, but you can only learn about them through the included examples and by looking at the source code. In particular, if you want to learn about the `Kinect()` object, which is the main interface for the device, you want to look at the source on GitHub:

`https://github.com/shiffman/libfreenect/blob/master/wrappers/java/processing/KinectProcess`
`ing/src/org/openkinect/processing/Kinect.java`

Here you'll see that the properties and methods associated with this object mostly deal with the depth and RGB data, like

```
enableDepth()
enableRGB()
getDepthImage()
getVideoImage()
getRawDepth()
etc.
```

▓ **Note** It's cool that there's also an interface here for the Kinect's motor control, so that if you call `tilt(15)`, your Kinect will tilt to 15 degrees! However, the motor inside the Kinect is not rated for continuous or even frequent use, and it will burn out, so use this feature judiciously.

Tweaking the Example

After you've played around with the example as is, let's try modifying it a bit. Specifically, let's tweak the `draw()` function and see what happens.

Higher Resolution

Only because it's stupid easy, the first thing we can do here is change the resolution as we did in Windows. You can see that the integer variable skip is used to skip over data points from the Kinect, because we just don't need every point to render a point cloud. Try changing

```
int skip = 4;
```

to

```
int skip = 1;
```

Rendering every single data point rather than every fourth data point will take its toll on the program's execution, which you'll notice in the slower frame rate when you run the sketch this time. Unlike on Windows, where our point cloud included RGB values, higher resolution here just means more "coverage" in the rendering, as in Figure 4-11.

Figure 4-11. *The pointcloud sketch at a higher resolution*

Depthmap and Thresholding

The pointcloud example looks cool and all, but much of the power of the Kinect and Kinect-like sensors is in the kinds of analysis they allow us to do in 3D space. If you skipped over the Windows section, you may have missed this point, so I will repeat myself verbatim: What really unlocks the power of the Kinect is the ability to selectively analyze the 3D space in front of the sensor, to pick out objects and people in the scene, and understand what's happening with them. What is the object? Is the person holding the object? Is the person gesturing? Such questions form a classic topic in machine vision known as scene analysis that has been extensively developed using 2D images over the past few decades. With the added depth information from a Kinect-like sensor or depth camera, scene analysis becomes much easier and more robust and the possibilities grow.

With that said, let's open the `RGBDepthTest` example, run it, and then tweak it to do some rudimentary scene analysis of our own.

Figure 4-12. The output of Shiffman's RGBDepthTest sketch

When you run the sketch and enable the RGB image by hitting "r," you'll see the RGB image and depth image—sometimes called a depthmap—side by side as in Figure 4-12. As you can imagine, programmatically picking out a region of interest in this scene is quite a bit easier and likely more accurate when we know at what depth we're looking for it.

So, let's do it. We're going to need to add a bit of code to the top of the sketch, as well as the `setup` and `draw` functions, to replace the depthmap with our own thresholded depth image.

Add these variable declarations to the top of the sketch to set the new depth image as well as the minimum and maximum depth to show. We will only draw pixels in this range, cutting out everything behind it.

```
PImage threshImage;
int minThresh =  0;
int maxThresh = 750;
```

Then provision the new depth image inside the `setup()` function:

```
void setup() {

  //...
```

Leave all the existing code intact and add

```
  threshImage = new PImage(640, 480);

}
```

Inside the `draw()` function, comment out the existing depth image renderer

```
//image(kinect.getDepthImage(),640,0);
```

Now add a routine inside the draw image to loop through all the depth pixels, setting any pixels within our threshold range to a color (blue) and everything else to black, as in the following:

```
int[] depth = kinect.getRawDepth();
  for (int i=0; i < 640*480; i++) {
    if (depth[i] > minThresh && depth[i] < maxThresh) {
      threshImage.pixels[i] = 0xFF0000FF;
    } else {
      threshImage.pixels[i] = 0;
    }
  }
}
```

Finally, draw our new depth image as follows:

```
threshImage.updatePixels();
image(threshImage, 640, 0);
```

When you run the sketch, you should see an output window like that shown in Figure 4-13.

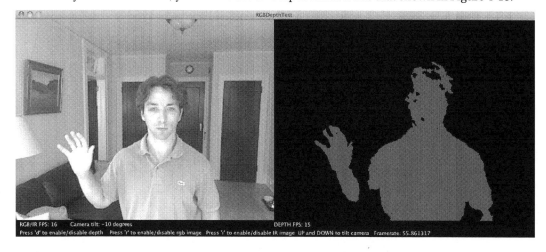

Figure 4-13. *Our thresholded depthmap as a model of the RGBDepthTest example sketch*

Thresholding the image at a given depth allows you to select out a slice in space, in this case grabbing a perfect outline of yourself at a given distance from the Kinect. Applying some of the traditional machine vision analysis and algorithms to this "blob" is what makes many of the Kinect applications go. In this chapter, we've just started down this long and fascinating path, building the foundation for such work in processing. Good job!

Processing Plus Kinect: Beyond This Book

It's beyond the scope of this book to delve into everything you can do with Processing plus Kinect, but if you're thinking Processing might be your tool of choice, there are some excellent resources out there on the open Web. One is SimpleOpenNI, a Processing wrapper for PrimeSense's OpenNI framework (covered in Chapter 6). SimpleOpenNI exposes in Processing all of the function calls and machine vision jujitsu that makes building a complex, gestural interface possible.

But don't leave this book with just Processing in your Kinect-hacking toolbox. There's much more out there. Depending on what you want to build or accomplish, you may be better served by another language or tool. In the next chapter, we survey the landscape of programming environments and frameworks that support Kinect hacking and try to show what hackers, artists, researchers, and visionaries in diverse domains have used to generate the veritable cornucopia of Kinect concoctions in the less than one year since the device's release.

CHAPTER 5

Kinect for Creatives

If you followed the explosion of hacker activity around the release of the Kinect, you noticed that many of the applications looked nothing like, say, Kinect Adventures for XBox. Armed with this revolutionary device, creative people of all stripes envisioned their own novel use cases: virtual puppets, 3D scan-and-print workflows, operating room image assistants, robots that see and follow people, gesture-controlled hovercraft, no-frills motion-capture Jedi animations, etc. How could such a diverse set of applications be possible?

The answer is in the accessibility of the Kinect to creative people: the mix of available software and development platforms that creators use within their own more specialized domains, whether visual arts, performance, robotics, or what have you. What follows is not a comprehensive list of these tools, but a selective inventory of some of the more popular and potentially useful ones and an overview of how to get started using the Kinect with them. These tools comprise a mix of free-and-open-source and proprietary commercial products, which run the gamut in terms of their respective learning curves. Processing, as discussed in the last chapter, may well be the right tool for the job if you're new to programming but want to learn and if the application of your dreams requires 2D or simple 3D animation, cross-platform support, and a smattering of its audio-visual and networking tools. In later chapters, we'll look closely at the more intensive, dedicated SDKs (software development kits) and development platforms for building rich gestural interfaces and 3D games—the kind of stuff you see, or will see, on XBox. In this chapter, we survey a different corner of the vast Kinect-hacking toolshed: the tools that creative coders (and non-coders) use to build all manner of projects, from Kinect-controlled musical instruments to full, motion-controlled Web apps. The idea is to present you, the reader, with the current breadth of tools available to execute your vision, whatever it is.

■ **Note** Subsequent chapters in this book discuss other frameworks and platforms, such as Beckon, Unity, OpenNI, and NITE. Those others are more general in nature and sometimes require deep programming expertise. The platforms described in this chapter are aimed specifically at the creative and artistic community.

MaxMSP

MaxMSP is more obscure than a mainstream software like Adobe Flash, but it's tailor-made for certain Kinect applications, for example those that involve the Kinect as an input to control sound or, say, stage lighting. Also, if you're a very visual person, or just really code-averse, you will want to check out MaxMSP.

MaxMSP does cost money. If you're on a budget or just prefer free software, you can look at MaxMSP's free-and-open-source competitor, PureData (PD). You can learn more about PureData at `http://puredata.info/`.

Patcher Programming Languages

MaxMSP and PD are sometimes called "patcher" programming languages because they let you patch together a bunch of pre-defined, graphical audio and video objects (including hardware), connecting and combining those objects with virtual patchcords and building your entire application without writing a line of code (though you can get under the hood and code if you want to).

That is *not* to say, however, that using a patcher language is necessarily any easier than writing code—you still have to understand the architecture of what you're trying to program. In fact, an argument can be made that patcher languages enforce good programming practice by forcing you to break down an application into so many discrete but connected parts. There is no doubt that for certain people and certain applications, patching is the way to go.

MaxMSP is a proprietary software, and a license will set you back about $400 (though significantly less for students), but as of this writing, there is better, more widely available support for using MaxMSP with Kinect than there is for PD.

What MaxMSP Can Do for You

MaxMSP is sometimes called just Max or Max/MSP/Jitter to denote all three components of the interactive programming environment from San Francisco–based Cycling '74. Despite shortening the name to MaxMSP for convenience, we shouldn't forget about Jitter! Jitter is the piece of the puzzle used for working with "matrices," a generic term for multidimensional data structures that include images and video (and therefore Kinect data). Like Processing, the whole MaxMSP package was created to support artists, educators, and researchers working intensively with audio-visual media and physical computing.

Digital artist Liubo Borissov's "hackiscan" was created using MaxMSP and a Kinect. Figure 5-1 shows the output of the hackiscan art installation. And in Figure 5-2, you can see how the application is set up inside the MaxMSP environment, which we'll explore in more detail later on.

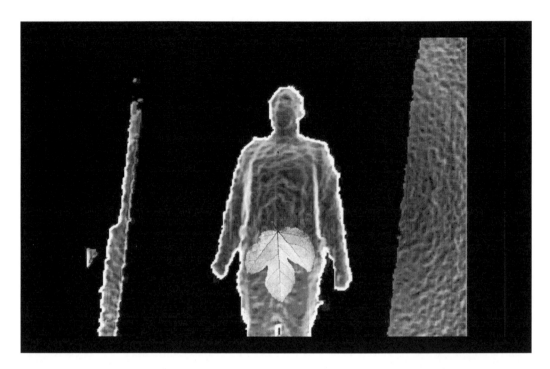

Figure 5-1. Digital artist Liubo Borissov's "hackiscan" ensures your privacy at the airport the old-fashioned way: with a fig leaf!

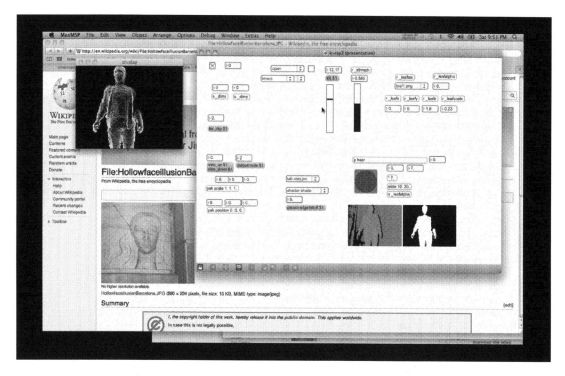

Figure 5-2. *Borissov's hackiscan project "under the hood" in the MaxMSP authoring environment—see the whole video online here: http://vimeo.com/17480291*

Getting Started: MaxMSP + Kinect

The best available technique for getting Kinect data into MaxMSP comes from Jean-Marc Pelletier as part of the broader OpenKinect project. Hit up Jean-Marc's GitHub repository for the latest code:

`https://github.com/jmpelletier/jit.freenect.grab`

Be sure to download the compiled "mex" and help files under Downloads>Download Packages on GitHub. Put the /jit folder somewhere special on your machine and launch the help file, i.e., the one with the extension .maxhelp. Now witness the plug-and-play magic of MaxMSP! Figure 5-3 shows what you'll see when you launch the help file.

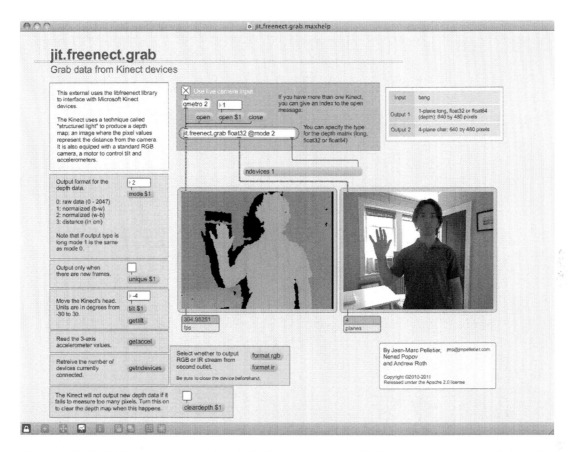

Figure 5-3. *The jit.freenect.grab.maxhelp help file presents you with Kinect data streams and a bunch of parameters to tweak on them.*

Check the "Use live camera input" box and click the "Open" button—you should see your Kinect data streaming in. This help interface lets you play with all kinds of variables: you can invert the coloration of the depthmap, for example, or tilt the Kinect's motor, like we did using RGBDemo.

Flash Actionscript

For those of us who cut our programming teeth on Adobe's (or way back when, Macromedia's) Flash Actionscript—as many Web and interactive designers did during the last decade—it is glorious news, indeed, to learn that several developer communities are actively working on connecting the Kinect to Flash. As of this writing, however, using the Kinect from Flash is not an easy row to hoe.

But wait, we keep hearing that Flash is dead, right? Why would we want to use it? It turns out that the rumors of Flash's demise are greatly exaggerated. Yes, HTML5 will replace some uses of Flash on the Web, such as for video. And yes, Flash is notoriously unsupported on Apple iOS devices because it enables the creation of rich, app-like interactive experiences right in the browser (which Apple can't charge for, thus undermining the App Store). But the Flash authoring environment is a powerful and intuitive integrated development environment (IDE) that thousands of Web designers and developers already know well. Flash's output, the SWF (pronounced "swiff") or Flash movie, is a highly optimized, Web-ready and cross-platform medium for rich video, animation, and interaction that will, no doubt, live on in its own right for at least a few years to come.

What Flash Can Do For You

So why would you want to use Flash for your Kinect application? Well, if you're going to be delivering it over the Web or using intensive 2D animation and interaction, or if you're already a Flash ninja, Flash plus Kinect may be just the combination for you.

Biltz Agency, a Los Angeles–based digital agency that produces cutting-edge media and marketing content for big brands, released a Kinect-to-Flash solution early in 2011 (more below) and demonstrated the proof-of-concept media browser shown in Figure 5-4.

Figure 5-4. *A Kinected media browser built in Flash by Blitz, a digital agency*

Getting Started: Flash + Kinect

As of this writing, the primary technique used to talk to Flash from the Kinect is to run a small helper app that grabs whatever data you want from the Kinect, does whatever low-level analysis you want to do on that data in a language like C or C++, and then sends along the information you plan to use in your application to Flash through a socket connection as if over a network connection. (In fact, it *can* be over a network connection, though you'll more likely run the socket server and your Flash movie on the same machine.)

Within the framework of this general approach, there is an important question to consider: How much of your Kinect data analysis do you want to do in Flash, and how much can you do before you send data on to Flash? As always, the answer is, "It depends."

What does it depend on? Well, a likely scenario for Flash application development is that you have an idea for an application that requires the hand-tracking, skeleton-tracking magic provided by extant machine vision libraries, like OpenCV or OpenNI/NITE. In that case, you're probably going to be in the camp of those who do a lot of data processing *before* sending anything to Flash, at which point you're sending some fairly minimal but powerful data, like the X-Y-Z coordinates of the hand-point tracked by NITE. The other alternative is to work with the Kinect's depth and RGB data directly in Flash, grabbing that data from the Kinect and hucking it over to your Flash movie for processing.

For the first alternative, the folks at Blitz Agency offer up a solution based on Node.js, a popular Javascript Web server. Blitz runs a modified version of one of the OpenNI/Nite sample applications called "SingleControl" and sends the pre-processed hand-point data over a socket to Flash using Node.js. Their steps are detailed on their development blog:

`http://labs.blitzagency.com/?p=2634`

Using this technique requires you to run three things at once, and it looks something like this: 1) start your socket server using Node.js and Blitz's JavaScript file which is configured to broadcast data at defined intervals (think "frames"); 2) run the modified SingleControl example to start collecting hand-point data and feeding it to the socket server; 3) run your Flash movie with a Socket object and a listener (ProgressEvent.SOCKET_DATA) to take some action whenever new handpoint data is received. Figure 5-5 shows how lean the data passed to Flash really is: much smaller than an RGB or depth image!

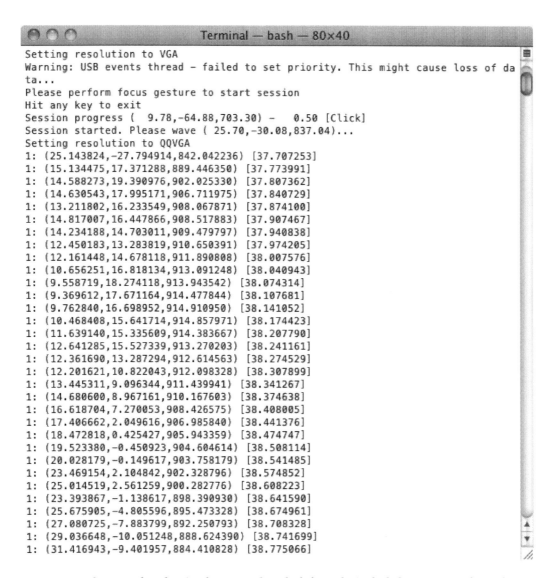

```
○ ○ ○                    Terminal — bash — 80×40
Setting resolution to VGA
Warning: USB events thread - failed to set priority. This might cause loss of da
ta...
Please perform focus gesture to start session
Hit any key to exit
Session progress (  9.78,-64.88,703.30) -   0.50 [Click]
Session started. Please wave ( 25.70,-30.08,837.04)...
Setting resolution to QQVGA
1: (25.143824,-27.794914,842.042236) [37.707253]
1: (15.134475,17.371288,889.446350) [37.773991]
1: (14.588273,19.390976,902.025330) [37.807362]
1: (14.630543,17.995171,906.711975) [37.840729]
1: (13.211802,16.233549,908.067871) [37.874100]
1: (14.817007,16.447866,908.517883) [37.907467]
1: (14.234188,14.703011,909.479797) [37.940838]
1: (12.450183,13.283819,910.650391) [37.974205]
1: (12.161448,14.678118,911.890808) [38.007576]
1: (10.656251,16.818134,913.091248) [38.040943]
1: (9.558719,18.274118,913.943542) [38.074314]
1: (9.369612,17.671164,914.477844) [38.107681]
1: (9.762840,16.698952,914.910950) [38.141052]
1: (10.468408,15.641714,914.857971) [38.174423]
1: (11.639140,15.335609,914.383667) [38.207790]
1: (12.641285,15.527339,913.270203) [38.241161]
1: (12.361690,13.287294,912.614563) [38.274529]
1: (12.201621,10.822043,912.098328) [38.307899]
1: (13.445311,9.096344,911.439941) [38.341267]
1: (14.680600,8.967161,910.167603) [38.374638]
1: (16.618704,7.270053,908.426575) [38.408005]
1: (17.406662,2.049616,906.985840) [38.441376]
1: (18.472818,0.425427,905.943359) [38.474747]
1: (19.523380,-0.450923,904.604614) [38.508114]
1: (20.028179,-0.149617,903.758179) [38.541485]
1: (23.469154,2.104842,902.328796) [38.574852]
1: (25.014519,2.561259,900.282776) [38.608223]
1: (23.393867,-1.138617,898.390930) [38.641590]
1: (25.675905,-4.805596,895.473328) [38.674961]
1: (27.080725,-7.883799,892.250793) [38.708328]
1: (29.036648,-10.051248,888.624390) [38.741699]
1: (31.416943,-9.401957,884.410828) [38.775066]
```

Figure 5-5. *The X-Y-Z hand-point data passed to Flash from the included NITE example application, SingleControl*

The OpenKinect-based AS3Kinect project pursues the second alternative, getting fairly raw data (images) from the Kinect and pumping it into Flash (again, using a socket server). Although this setup also requires a fair bit of diligence, it can be well worth it if you're itching to train your Flash/Actionscript 3 chops on a Kinect project. Details about the AS3Kinect project can be found here:

http://www.as3kinect.org/

openFrameworks

Unlike the other tools profiled in this chapter—and, in fact, most of the rest of this book—neither openFrameworks nor Cinder (the next project profiled) provides you with a self-contained environment for writing and compiling code. As the "openFrameworks" name implies, they are simply "frameworks," or bunches of pre-written code you can use to handle common tasks in the otherwise daunting languages of C++ and OpenGL. C++ and OpenGL are two relatively old and extremely powerful languages with which you can build very robust interactive desktop and mobile applications. C++ is your low-level, functional programming language, while OpenGL handles your high-performance 2D and 3D graphics processing and rendering.

As with Processing and Cinder (as we'll see) openFrameworks is built to support intuitive, sketch-style "creative coding," a domain that includes all the things that interactive artists, designers, and application developers might want to do with graphics, media, data, and hardware.

That turns out to be a lot of things. The openFrameworks project, which began as a collaboration between Zach Lieberman and Theodore Watson at Parsons School of Design, has grown to become a vast and powerful library used by thousands of installation artists, performers, and hackers.

What openFrameworks Can Do for You

The openFrameworks community, which has forever had a hand in creative computer vision applications, jumped right into the Kinect hacking frenzy. Why? The Kinect and Kinect-like sensors help solve one of the fundamental challenges of creating interactive, vision-based applications: namely, getting a clear picture of what the user is doing. Moreover, the Kinect can be powerfully combined with some of the other tools built into or wrapped by openFrameworks. OpenCV, the computer vision library discussed in the last chapter, is a great example. Whereas OpenCV can be used to accomplish tough computer vision tasks, like face detection or recognition, those tasks become easier when combined with the ability to see in 3D and, say, know roughly where to look in the image for faces. With openFrameworks, we can bring both of these technologies under the same roof, so to speak, and do some amazing stuff. One of the first demonstrations of the possibilities was the interactive puppet prototype created by Design I/O's Emily Gobeille and openFrameworks co-creator Theo Watson, as shown in Figure 5-6.

Figure 5-6. *A projected virtual puppet application built with openFrameworks by Emily Gobeille and Theo Watson*

Getting Started: openFrameworks + Kinect

Like C++ and OpenGL themselves, openFrameworks works cross-platform and can be used on PC, Mac, and Linux. However, you have to supply your own integrated development environment (IDE), the authoring environment that lets you pull together all the files of the frameworks and compile them along with your own code. Supported IDEs for openFrameworks are Code::Blocks on all platforms, plus Visual C++ 2008 and Visual C++ 2010 on Windows and Xcode on Mac.

Once you're set up with your IDE of choice, you'll need to go to the website to pull down the latest release of openFrameworks, which is 0.07 as of this writing. (Not a reference to James Bond, as far as we know!) Here is the URL to visit:

`http://www.openframeworks.cc/download`

Grabbing the latest release of openFrameworks for your intended platform and IDE should give you sample projects inside the apps/examples folder that you can open and build to make sure everything is set up. If you do that and get a number of compatibility and "file not found" errors, welcome: this is your initiation to working with frameworks! Not to worry, it's very common to have to poke around following error codes when you first start compiling your own programs from source code. Stay with it! The openFrameworks examples, in particular, use relative addressing to pull in files and frameworks; so if you try to compile a project that you have sitting in the wrong folder, it will certainly break.

Once you've successfully compiled a few of the basic examples, it's time to try some Kinect stuff. For working from scratch with the libfreenect driver, Theo Watson released an "add-on" (the preferred term for an optional module or plugin) called ofxKinect, which wraps the libfreenect driver for use in openFrameworks. Grab the add-on from `https://github.com/ofTheo/ofxKinect`.

Just download that project, move it to the /add-ons folder, move the example project to the apps/examples folder, open the example project, and compile it. You can toggle between a kind of feedback dashboard, shown in Figure 5-7, and the now-familiar pointcloud, shown in Figure 5-8. What's especially powerful about openFrameworks is its easy integration with that deep computer vision library, OpenCV. As you can see in Figure 5-7, the bottom left feedback image is a depthmap, but now has some additional analysis to detect the "blob" (i.e., the author) in the scene, courtesy of OpenCV. Blob detection is indicated by rectangles drawn over the image.

Figure 5-7. *The ofxKinect example project shows a depthmap, RGB image, and blob detection*

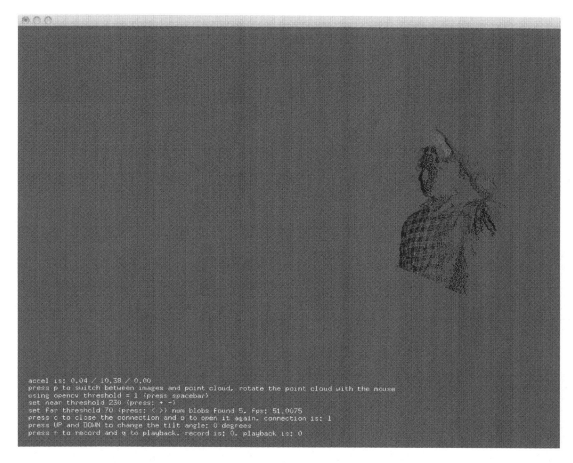

Figure 5-8. The ofxKinect example project would not be complete without showing a pointcloud view of the data

Alternatively, if you want to use OpenNI's pre-built abstraction layer and algorithmic magic, like hand and skeletal tracking, Diederick Huijbers, a Dutch artist/developer and prolific contributor to openFrameworks, released an add-on for openFrameworks that wraps OpenNI, called ofxOpenNI. Get that add-on here:

```
https://github.com/roxlu/ofxOpenNI
```

Cinder

Much of what we've said above about openFrameworks can also be said about Cinder, a C++ framework for "creative coding" that was released by The Barbarian Group digital agency in 2010. Cinder is a newer project and probably a tad scarier than openFrameworks for the C++ newbie. There's a great deal of overlap between the two projects, and comparing them point for point would require lots of space and quite a bit of subtlety about things like design philosophy and C++ memory management. Suffice it to say that both projects bear consideration if you're looking to create a slick C++ app.

What Cinder Can Do For You

So, why use Cinder for your Kinect app? The work created using Cinder speaks for itself. Simply put, it can help you do awe-inspiring graphical work and push the envelope visually. Add in a depth-seeing camera and you have the makings of a Roman orgy of interactive visual delights! As mentioned in Chapter 3, digital artist Robert Hodgins's "Body Dysmorphia" was created using Cinder and demonstrates some of the downright disturbing 3D visual effects that are possible. (Hodgins himself is a co-creator of Cinder.) As shown in Figure 5-9, if the camera adds ten pounds, the Kinect plus Cinder adds ten pounds and then some!

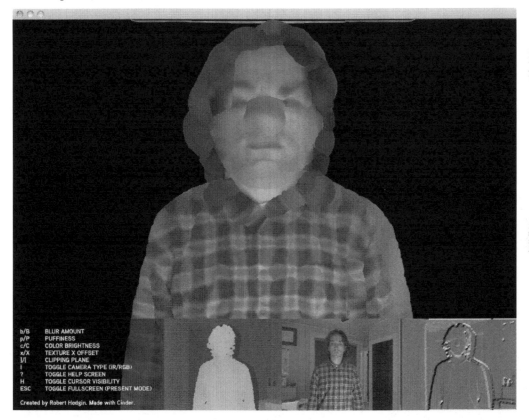

Figure 5-9. *The Cinder-based Body Dysmorphia project by digital artist Robert Hodgins*

Getting Started With Cinder

As with openFrameworks—or any frameworks, for that matter—you need to supply the IDE. Cinder will work with Visual C++ 2008 and Visual C++ 2010 on Windows and with Xcode on Mac. As of this writing, though, it does not play well with Linux.

So, just download the latest release of Cinder and put it somewhere—anywhere. You can pull down the code from here:

`http://libcinder.org/download/`

Again, it's a good idea to build one or two of the out-of-the-box examples inside the /samples folder. If everything seems to build okay, it's time to rock the Kinect with Cinder.

Kinect support for Cinder doesn't come in a "block" (the preferred term for an optional module or plugin) but in a couple of samples and supporting files from Hodgins, aptly named Cinder-Kinect. Get these files here:

`https://github.com/cinder/Cinder-Kinect`

Cinder-Kinect wraps the libfreenect driver and is currently the only available option for making your Kinect data available to Cinder. Download Cinder-Kinect and drop the whole folder (including the /include, /lib, /samples, and /src folders) into the main Cinder /samples folder. This should ensure that any relative locations used in the project files work. When you build the kinectBasic example, you get the depth and RGB images from the Kinect.

And when you build the kinectPointCloud example, you get yet another variation on the 3D point cloud. Though in our opinion, this is one of the most pleasing to the eye and interesting, in terms of the level of detail it surfaces.

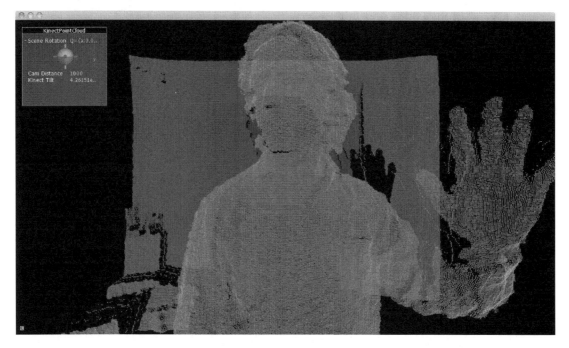

Figure 5-10. *Cinder-Kinect's version of the pointcloud*

Now, Go Forth and Create!

In this chapter, we wanted to briefly introduce you to the palette of tools available for creative coding with the Kinect. Each of these tools deserves a book of its own! If you choose one of them for your project, you'll no doubt need to explore it in a bit more depth (no pun intended!). Our modest hope is that now, as your ideas for awesome, creative Kinect projects arise, you'll be that much better equipped to find the right tool for the job having read this chapter. In the next chapter, we turn to some of the most powerful and popular general development frameworks for Kinect. Onward!

CHAPTER 6

Application Development with the Beckon Framework

Up until this point, we have covered open source platforms that work with Kinect. In addition to these tools, other advanced commercial frameworks are available to explore. These suites can provide additional tools, applications, and functionality. One exciting platform is Omek Interactive's Beckon Development Suite. Omek's Beckon SDK performs skeleton tracking, gesture recognition, and blob tracking, and it also comes with a suite of tools for recording custom gestures with the Kinect and many of the other 3D sensor cameras currently available. These new gestures can then be used in any application created with the Beckon SDK. For example, if you want to make a painting program, you can design gestures specific to your application. In this chapter, we'll go through the basic Flash example included with Beckon, we'll create a simple skeleton, and then we'll train our own gesture. We will then integrate both the skeleton and trained gesture into a basic application. Using Flash with Beckon creates a standalone application rather than a browser compatible .swf file. We will cover the use of Beckon with Flash because of Flash's capability for rapid prototyping of environments. As we go along, we'll also discuss basic UX design strategies for gesture interfaces.

Note The .swf files are compiled Flash files. They originally were referred to as "Shockwave Flash Files", but are today commonly referred to only by their extension .swf. The type of application you get using Beckon with Flash is a stand-alone Flash application of the type stored in a .fla file.

What is Beckon?

Omek Interactive, a breakthrough company based in Israel, created Beckon. Their aim was to transform the way people interact with their devices and applications, by providing tools and technology that enable manufacturers and software developers to add gesture-based interfaces to their products. Beckon is perhaps the most robust SDK covered in this book. Beckon is part middleware and part toolbox. Middleware is a piece of software that sits between one application or hardware device and another one. Up until this point in the book, you've been using either OpenNI and NITE or the Microsoft SDK to extrapolate and analyze the data coming in from your Kinect. Beckon is unique in that it supports nearly all of the depth cameras on the market (and has plans to support future cameras). By leveraging a proprietary machine learning environment, Beckon allows developers and designers to create completely customized interactive applications and immersed environments in Adobe Flash CS 5.5, C++ or C#, as well as plug-ins for the .NET framework and the Unity and OGRE game engines. It is fully compatible with any game engine and natively supports the industry-standard FBX animation format for blending pre-generated 3Dcontent with real-time tracking.

The Beckon API provides what it refers to as "scene intelligence" at the blob, skeleton, or gesture level. The Basic and GUI Gesture Packs provide predefined, ready-to-use gestures for different contexts (UI control, game control, etc.). Developers can easily integrate these Gesture Packs into their applications.

Designers can also record completely original gestures, or gesture combinations, for their applications using the applications that come with Beckon. The Gesture Authoring Toolkit is a suite of tools that allows both designers and developers to define and manage their own gestures, and even to create new gestures without writing code. Gestures can be very intuitive and combined together. In music creation software, a gesture for a musician to loop a track might be drawing a circle in space. With a first person martial arts game, perhaps a jump and a dodge are the right moves for a player to escape a punch from an opponent.

Beckon's machine learning environment can learn from many different samples of the same gesture. Creating a gesture is a process of performing and recording it in front of the camera several times. This process is referred to as training the machine learning environment. Machine learning is a branch of Artificial Intelligence and is nothing to be afraid of. Simply put, the computer learns through recorded gestures and gets better at recognizing the gesture with each new sample. Beckon allows designers and developers to get highly accurate recognition, even across diverse populations. For example, the way that a 12 year old boy and a 30 year old woman will look making the same gesture is quite different. Beckon allows your program to identify both users with ease. While Beckon is a great tool over all, it's this feature that sets it a head above other technology specialized for Kinect.

Kinect, like any other sensor, requires the installation of a separate device driver built by the community. Currently, the most popular solution is the SensorKinect, an open source project based on the PrimeSensor device driver. It's important to understand that the SensorKinect drivers cannot co-exist with the standard PrimeSensor drivers on the same PC, because the SensorKinect drivers were designed to make the Kinect sensor appear as a standard PrimeSensor device. For this reason, we'd recommend adding a new OS onto a blank partition on your hard drive and booting from there so that you can switch back to other SDKs later. For this chapter, we will be using Windows 7; however, XP also works. Because of the need to uninstall your drivers, you might want to read this chapter first to decide if Beckon suits your needs.

▓ **Note** Beckon is currently available via a 90-day free trial evaluation version; however, Omek will be providing a non-commercial version to the public with their next major release. If you would like to get your hands on a copy now, you can request a copy here: www.omekinteractive.com/beckon-eval or by contacting the team at info@omekinteractive.com. While you can't purchase a license directly from Omek's website, you can contact their sales team, who will provide you with details on how to get a commercial version of their SDK. Pricing depends on the type of application you are looking to commercialize, so it's best to reach out to them for details. On the upside, not only does Beckon work with Kinect, but it also works with the Panasonic D-Imager, the Asus Xtion Pro, PMDTec's GameCube 3.0, and the PMD[vision] CamCube. You'll also get access to the incredible support team, who will ensure that you get the installation functional on your platform.

Speaking based on personal use, this platform performs flawlessly and Beckon's stability cannot be overstated. I've seen it seamlessly track a player in a game with as many as 40 people standing directly behind that person, cheering and taking photos. It also does a very good job at allowing one person to leave a game and another to enter into the Kinect's view and start playing. It will register the player change and start tracking within seconds, with no calibration poses. Shockingly accurate, it was able to recognize people as young as 2 and as old as 70+ years of age performing the same gestures. The performance that Beckon delivers makes it worth the investment.

Regardless of the initial setup time, if you're interested in developing a game or application simultaneously for iOS, Android, touch display, and Kinect, Beckon really is a timesaver. Otherwise, you'd have to have to build the iOS application in Objective C, the Droid version in Java, and the Kinect version a language like C++. Plus, it's fun, as a game developer, to be able to take a game to a festival and set it up to run in a kiosk version making use of the Kinect. Beckon makes this very easy to do.

If you're scratching your head right now and thinking, "I heard Flash didn't run on an iPad!" welcome to the new version of Flash, CS 5.5, which supports multiscreen output natively from both Flash and Flash Builder. The number one best-selling apps on the iTunes store are now made with Flash, such as the heavily awarded Machinarium. Great tips are available for developing this way online. A good place to start is the games section of the Adobe site here: `www.adobe.com/devnet/games.html`.

Installing Beckon

Kinect, like any other sensor, requires the installation of a separate device driver. To this end, we rely on public components written by the Kinect-developers community. The most popular solution is SensorKinect, an open source project based on the PrimeSensor device driver. It's important to understand that SensorKinect drivers cannot co-exist with the standard PrimeSensor drivers on the same PC, because SensorKinect drivers were designed to make the Kinect sensor appear as a standard PrimeSensor device.

Getting Beckon up and running takes a few steps. I recommend checking the Omek website for the most up-to-date details, since the appropriate drivers will change as Omek releases updates and newer versions of their software. The first thing you are going to need to do is to remove the Open NI SDK and PrimeSense drivers you currently have on your OS An additional word to the wise is that you will also need to make sure that you fully uninstall and remove from your system your libfreenect open Kinect drivers. Failing to do so will cause Beckon to be unable to recognize the sensor camera. Afterwards, we will re-download and install versions of OpenNI and the PrimSense drivers that are appropriate for Beckon. Finally, we will install the Beckon SDK and license and get started.

▓ **Note** If you are a developer possibly coming over from the Mac OS and want to take full advantage of the SDK, you'll want to make sure you have Visual Studio Professional and the .NET framework installed as well.

Step 1: Remove Existing Drivers

The first step is to remove any existing drivers on your system that might conflict with the Beckon software or the drivers needed to run that software. Some drivers are removed from the Control Panel. Others are removed from the Windows Device Manager. Here is what to do for the Control Panel drivers:

1. Go to Start -> Settings -> Control Panel
2. Select the Programs Control Panel

3. Select the "Uninstall a Program" option

4. Uninstall any application having "OpenNI" or "PrimeSense" in their name. Examples include: OpenNI 1.0.0, PrimeSensor 5.0.0 for Windows, Windows Driver Package – PrimeSense (psdrv3) PrimeSensor, etc.

The following shows how to use Device Driver to remove drivers:

1. Go to Start -> Computer

2. Right-click on Computer, and choose Manage

3. Click on Device Manager

4. Open Human Interface Devices

5. Find XBox NUI Camera, right-click, and choose Uninstall

6. Find XBox NUI Motor and XBox NUI Camera drivers, right-click, and uninstall those too

Step 2: Install New Drivers

Now that any possibly conflicting other software and drivers are out of the way, you can download and install what Beckon needs. Here are the instructions to follow:

1. Download the OpenNI 1.0.0.25 installer.

2. Download and install the SensorKinect 5.0.0 drivers.

3. Install OpenNI by running the installer downloaded in #1.

4. Install SensorKinect by running the installer downloaded in #2.

▓ **Note** Check the example download for this book for possibly new information regarding driver installation.

Step 3: Download and Install the Beckon SDK

Now it's time to download and install the Beckon SDK. It's best to use either Internet Explorer or Firefox for that purpose, especially if you have a firewall installed. Here is the process to follow:

1. Navigate to the customer service portal at:
   https://license.omekinteractive.com/solo/customers/Default.aspx

2. Log in using the customer ID and password provided to you by Omek and download your license. Omek will email you this when they agree to give you a license. See the Omek Beckon SDK Installation Guide if you get lost here.

3. Download the Beckon SD. Using the link provided in the email you received from Beckon when you signed up for a non-commercial license, install the software. The only tricky popup to watch out for will be the final popup in the

process, shown in Figure 6-1. If you have a Windows7 64 bit system with Visual C++ installed, press "No." Otherwise, press "Yes."

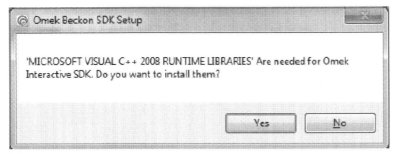

Figure 6-1. *The Beckon installer's final, but tricky, popup.*

Activating Beckon

Beckon SDK is license protected; you have 3 days to activate your license. Run the Tracking Viewer tool to activate the software according to your license permissions. You'll find that tool from your Start menu, at Start -> Omek Beckon -> Tracking Viewer. Don't run it quite yet, though.

First, plug in your Kinect device. Driver installation is part of the validation process.

Now run the Tracking Viewer. Beckon will walk you through the validation process. You will see a popup notification that will let you know the drivers for Kinect are installing. You will see the Xbox NUI Audio driver fail. This is perfectly normal and a sign that you have done everything correctly to this point.

■ **Note** The Omek Beckon SDK Installation Guide provides a simple step by step guide if you need more help.

Getting Started

Now we are going to see whether our installation was successful. The Beckon installation includes a sample application that you can use to test for a successful install. From the Start Menu, launch "Omek BeckonTracking Viewer"

Note For reference, the executable is located in the following folder: C:/ Program Files/Omek/Beckon SDK/ bin/ Omek Beckon Tracking Viewer.exe

In the Omek Beckon Tracking Viewer, choose: Open -> Live Camera. If everything is installed, you will see something similar to Figure 6-2.

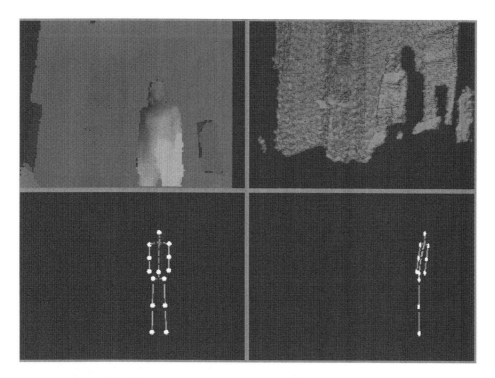

Figure 6-2. *Omek Beckon Tracking Viewer*

Incorporating Beckon with Flash

Now let's use the Beckon SDK in Flash. Again, Flash with Beckon creates standalone applications, not browser experiences. Beckon will not work in a browser with Flash or online; you don't actually install Beckon as a flash library or load it as a .swc file. However, the beat on the street is that this is the last version of Beckon that does not include an embedded solution. The process for Beckon is different. The way Beckon works with Flash is through Flash's ExternalInterface. You create your flash file and expose functions that will communicate with the Beckon SDK. Beckon has another application, "OmekBeckonFlash.exe" that communicates between the running swf file and the Beckon library. Beckon uses an xml file, config.xml, to tell the BeckonFlash application where to look for the swf to run. It also sets some of the initial start settings.

To run the Beckon Flash example, do the following:

1. Create a new folder for the project (e.g., C:\MyProject)

2. Copy the necessary files from "C:\Program Files\Omek\Beckon SDK\bin" to C:\MyProject. You can either follow the instructions on the Developer Guide, under "Distribution of Omek-Based Content", or simply copy everything from inside the bin folder to your project's folder.

3. Copy "C:\Program Files\Omek\Beckon SDK\samples\Flash" to C:\MyProject. Make sure to name the target folder "Flash", and with a capital "F".

4. Run OmekBeckonFlash.exe

5. Now the Flash example .swf will open in this application, and it will run linked to the Omek SDK.

At this point, you should see something similar to Figure 6-3. This is not a browser but a separate, standalone application

Figure 6-3. Default stand-alone Flash example running in OmekBeckonFlash.exe

The following is how Beckon communicates with Flash:

1. OmekBeckonFlash.exe loads the Flash/config.xml (you must keep this name)

2. The Flash project is loaded from the path, specified in the config.xml, in the `<movie swfPath=".\Flash\game.swf" />` tag.

3. The SDK is loaded and uses the exposed function in the .swf file to send data to the running .swf file.

You should now be up and running with the Beckon SDK.

■ **Note** Omek is currently streamlining the process of running Flash applications, so expect improvements. Expect to see rapid updates, quick changes, and innovation.

Understanding the Beckon Flash Example

Before we create our own Flash file, let's explore the Beckon Flash example. By understanding how Beckon's example works, you will be equipped to create a project from scratch.

How Beckon Works with Flash

Before we even open Flash, we are going to do a basic walk-through of two lines of code so that we can get the hang of how Beckon works with Flash. If you are used to working with Flash, you might be used to seeing the `ExternalInterface.callback()` class. Using the ExternalInterface class, you can call an ActionScript function in the Flash runtime environment. Usually, this class is used so that a running swf file can communicate with JavaScript in a Browser. However, in this case, Beckon uses an additional application, OmekBeckonFlash.exe, to run the swf file within. Because functions are exposed in the .swf file, the OmekBeckonFlash application can send information from SDK to them.

We are going to look at two key methods of ExternalCalllback class. The first is `.addCallback`. This method registers an ActionScript method as callable from the container swf.

Here's the whole line of code that is in the Flash file.

```
ExternalInterface.addCallback("OmekGesture", onOmekGesture);
```

This addCallback method exposes onOmekGesture to the sdk.

The next method call passes arguments from the .swf file to the OmekBeckonFlash application. The call sets up two way communications between Flash and Beckon. It also tells the OmekAddGesture function to register the leftPush gesture if it is performed in the camera's view. Here's the relevant line of code:

```
ExternalInterface.call("OmekAddGesture","leftPush");
```

Now that we have established how Beckon works with Flash, let's look at the actual Flash file. Open `C:\MyProject\Flash\testOmekFlashPlayer` in Flash. You will see the basic interface that ran when we started the OmekBeckonFlash.exe file. That's because parts of the interface were created within Flash. Note that no box exists for the RGB video feed or for the depth map. This is because these elements are added into the file through the config.xml file. Beckon uses both Flash and this file to set up the start parameters for the OmekBeckonFlash application.

You can change a few things in the code to help you understand what is happening. First, resize the text box on the stage labeled `debugString_txt` so that you can actually see all of the debug code that is written there when BeckonFlash.exe runs the swf file. Resize it to be the size of the entire stage and make the text about 10pt in size. You can go ahead and also make it white. Now set your background color to black to make it easy to read. Save and export the application.

Now run the example again. Move around and you will see all of the debug copy writing to screen, as shown in Figure 6-4.

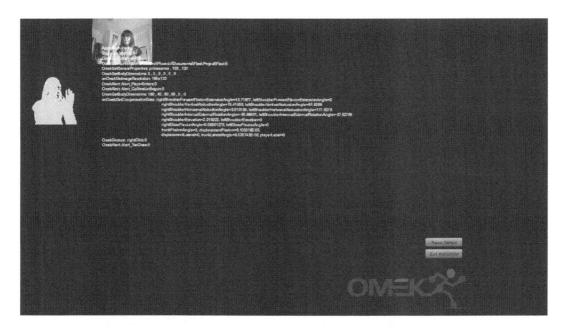

Figure 6-4. *Modified stand alone Flash example running in OmekBeckonFlash.exe*

The greatest difficulty working with Flash and Beckon is the loss of a console window. You could use brute force and drop a text box onto the screen and send messages to it, but a cleaner way to get debug text on screen is to create a function that draws debug text via Actionscript.

Notice how the example now reflects the above changes. I triggered a few of the functions that are in the file by performing gestures or causing alerts to display on screen. Try doing the same by moving to close to the Kinect or walking out of view. You will now see all of the new lines being written to screen. They were there before, but because the textbox was so small, you didn't see the debug text being displayed. Now you can easily in the debugString_txt box's text.

I perform the right click gesture in Figure 6-4. Performing this gesture is just a matter of tapping forward with a quick double-tap like motion as your right hand is slightly raised in front of you to about chest height. It's the same motion you'd make to tap someone on the shoulder who was sitting directly in front of you. The debug text shows this gesture was seen by the camera and registered. Next, I intentionally got to close to the camera to trigger the "Alert_TooClose" alert.

The reason the debugString_txt box is important is that, by running the swf in a 3rd party application, you lose access to the normal console window in Flash. Creating messages that appear on-screen for debugging purposes is a fundamental change that you are going to have to adapt to when working with Beckon. A smart way to handle this is to create a debug mode in your application that you can trigger with a keystroke to turn onscreen alerts on or off.

The Example Code

Now, let's look at the code for Beckon's Flash example. To look at the code, open the Actions panel and look at the Actionscript on the first frame of the timeline.

▓ **Note** Choose Windows > Actions from the menu to view the actions panel.

You should see an import at the top of the code. You are going to want to import the following class in every Flash application you create using the Beckon SDK:

```
import flash.external.ExternalInterface;
```

Next up is the ExternalInterface code that exposes specified functions to the swf file. Step one is always to expose the function to the Flash runtime environment. Step two is optional, and sends messages to set up the functionality from the `ExternalInterface.call` method. The last step then is to setup the exposed function.

Admittedly, this process of exposing functions feels like a hack. Without a doubt, it would be best if Omek would build a version the Beckon sdk as a flash library so it could be released easily online, or distributed to other people with a Kinect. For now, you are locked into the one system on which you have running your specific copy of Beckon. Hopefully, this situation will change with future releases of the Beckon sdk.

Three of the `ExternalInterface.callback()` methods in the action script are mandatory and must be implemented in every file planning to use Beckon. Each integrates some basic functionally. We will review these three mandatory methods and the functions they expose. Others are optional, but the three we cover in this chapter are mandatory.

We cover the three methods out of the order that they are used in the ActionScript file. We cover them in the order that we do because this allows us to explain the code more clearly. We'll refer to the ActionScript code by line number to make the discussion as easy to follow as we can.

Line 8 takes care of handling gestures by exposing the function onOmekGesture in the flash runtime.

```
ExternalInterface.addCallback("OmekGesture", onOmekGesture);
```

The next method to look at is on line 56. This method lets the sdk know to register the leftPush gesture. This gesture is a gesture included in the sdk. Each gesture that a user wants to detect must be listed here, including custom gestures.

```
ExternalInterface.call("OmekAddGesture","leftPush");
```

Now, review the exposed function onOmekGesture on line 106.

```
function onOmekGesture(gestureName:String, playerLabel:String):void
{
        debugString_txt.appendText("\nOmekGesture: " + gestureName + ":" + playerLabel);
}
```

This function can receive two strings from the SDK. The first is the name of the gesture received and the next is the label of the player. Beckon can track multiple players and easily switch between them. It supports up to 5 players. It can also track an unlimited number of what it refers to as candidates, or possible players.

Skeleton Data

Next, let's look at how to handle getting skeleton data into flash. Line 9 exposes the function onOmekJointPosition:

```
ExternalInterface.addCallback("OmekJointPosition", onOmekJointPosition);
```

You must list every joint you would like to receive, but not in the Flash file. Open the Config.html file. This file is located in this folder: `C:\MyProject\Flash`. Open the file and take note of the `<tracking>` tag. Its contents should appear as follows:

```
<tracking>
            <skeleton rawSkeleton="true"/>
            <joint name="rightFingerTip" screen="false" smooth="true"/>
            <joint name="leftFingerTip" screen="false" smooth="true"/>
            <joint name="torso" screen="false" smooth="true"/>
</tracking>
```

This `<tracking>` tag registers all of the joints to be tracked. You *must* list each joint that you want to track. In this example, only the left and right fingertips and the torso are tracked. Since this tag sets up the joints ahead of time in this xml file, there's no need to use .call to send messages to the SDK.

Joint Positions

Now let's look at the onOmekJointPosition function. It receives a joint's name, the playerLabel associated with the joint, and the X,Y,Z position of the joint in space. Here's the code from the example:

```
function onOmekJointPosition(jointName:String, playerLabel:String, jointX:String,
jointY:String, jointZ:String, confidence:String):void
{
//give control on mouses to one specific player.
if(playerLabel == "0")
{
  if(jointName == "leftFingerTip")
  {
  //mirror X value in order to make the mouse move left and right like the hand.
  leftFingerTip_mc.x = stage.stageWidth - Number(jointX) * _screenScaleX + _correctionX;
  leftFingerTip_mc.y = Number(jointY) * _screenScaleY + _correctionY;

  //debugString_txt.appendText("\nleftFingerTip_mc located at:
  //("+leftFingerTip_mc.x.toString()+","+leftFingerTip_mc.y.toString()+")");
  }
  if(jointName == "rightFingerTip")
  {
  rightFingerTip_mc.x = stage.stageWidth - Number(jointX) * _screenScaleX + _correctionX;
  rightFingerTip_mc.y = Number(jointY) * _screenScaleY + _correctionY;
  }
  }
}
```

This function gives player 0 control and attaches to the circle graphic movie clips, `leftFingerTip_mc` and `rightFingerTip_mc`, to the longest finger point of each hand. This function also prints the location of these joints to the `debugString_txt` box on the stage.

Beckon can track multiple players and it assigns each player a number. The first player is player 0.

Alerts

The last mandatory functionality is to handle Alerts. On line 10, notice the onOmekAlert function is exposed to the Flash runtime environment:

```
ExternalInterface.addCallback("OmekAlert", onOmekAlert);
```

Each alert that you want to listen for must also be sent to the SDK with a .call method. On lines 62-79 a partial list of the alert listeners that are available are sent to the sdk with each corresponding message to listen for, starting with the following line:

```
ExternalInterface.call("OmekAddAlert","Alert_CalibrationDone");
```

Let's look at the exposed onOmekAlert function now and see what it does:

```
function onOmekAlert(alertName:String, playerLabel:String):void
{
debugString_txt.appendText("\nOmekAlert: " + alertName + ":" + playerLabel);

if (alertName =="Alert_CalibrationDone"){
//only after Alert_CalibrationDone the OmekGetBodyDimensions will return the correct values
  ExternalInterface.call("OmekGetBodyDimensions","0");
  //ask for the body compensation of a specific player. return a value to
ExternalInterface.addCallback("OmekGetCompensationData", onOmekGetCompensationData);
  ExternalInterface.call("OmekGetCompensationData","0");
} else if (alertName == "Alert_CalibrationBegun"){
  ExternalInterface.call("OmekGetBodyDimensions","0");
  //ask for the body compensation of a specific player. return a value to
  //ExternalInterface.addCallback("OmekGetCompensationData", onOmekGetCompensationData);
  ExternalInterface.call("OmekGetCompensationData","0");
}
```

This function handles a few alerts. For each one, it just prints copy to the debugString_txt field. Nothing fancy happens here. A handy use for this function in the future would be to display player warnings on screen.

The Core Functionality

We are now finished with the code needed to set up Beckon Flash integration. Now that we have covered the most basic setup, let's look at how the functionality we've talked about is integrated into our example. First, the code checks to see if a sensor is connected and ready. If the sensor is ready to use and everything is hooked up, all of the appropriate queries are then sent to the sdk. This process starts on line 21 with an addEventListener running every frame to see if the sensor is ready. Here is the relevant code, beginning from line 21:

```
//wait for connecting to the sensor before querying it.
addEventListener(Event.ENTER_FRAME,checkIfSensorReady);
function checkIfSensorReady(e:Event):void
{
//ask if the sensor is ready to receive queries. return a value to
//ExternalInterface.addCallback("OmekIsSensorConnected", onOmekIsSensorConnected);
ExternalInterface.call("OmekIsSensorConnected","");
}
```

Notice the next function, onOmekIsSensorConnected, is now exposed to the sdk and the OmekIsSensorConnected function in the SDK is triggered by .call and receives false or true.

The onOmekIsSensorConnected function receives a string from the SDK. If it is the string true, the function sendQueriesToSensor runs.

```
/**
 * function returns true or false if the sensor is connected.
 *
 * connected : boolean (as a string) "true" or "false", marking if the sensor is ready
 */
function onOmekIsSensorConnected(connected:String):void
{
  if ( connected=="true" )
  {
    removeEventListener(Event.ENTER_FRAME,checkIfSensorReady);
    sendQueriesToSensor();
  }
}
```

Next is the function sendQueriesToSensor. This is the function that sends all of the call messages to the SDK. (sendQueriesToNSensor also exposes a few more functions). This is important because these calls include all gestures to be tracked and all alert messages to send. For example:

```
function sendQueriesToSensor():void
{
  //set the number of players the sensor tracks
  ExternalInterface.call("OmekSetMaxPlayers","2");
  //ask for the tracked number of players. return a value to
  //ExternalInterface.addCallback("OmekGetMaxPlayers", onOmekGetMaxPlayers);
  ExternalInterface.call("OmekGetMaxPlayers","");

  //set the sensor's tracking mode to either: "all", "basic", "upper", or "sitting"
  ExternalInterface.call("OmekSetTrackingMode","all");
  //ask for the current tracking mode. return a value to
  //ExternalInterface.addCallback("OmekGetTrackingMode", onOmekGetTrackingMode);
  ExternalInterface.call("OmekGetTrackingMode","");

  //adding listeners for the sensor to specific gestures (see documentation
  //for full list of gestures available)
  ExternalInterface.call("OmekAddGesture","leftPush");
  ExternalInterface.call("OmekAddGesture","rightClick");
  ExternalInterface.call("OmekAddGesture","jumpNoHands");
  //removing listeners from the sensor to specific gestures
  ExternalInterface.call("OmekRemoveGesture","leftPush");

  //adding listeners to specific alerts (see documentation for full
  //list of alerts available).
  ExternalInterface.call("OmekAddAlert","Alert_CalibrationDone");
  ExternalInterface.call("OmekAddAlert","Alert_CalibrationBegun");
  ExternalInterface.call("OmekAddAlert","Alert_TooClose");
  ExternalInterface.call("OmekAddAlert","Alert_TooFar");
  ExternalInterface.call("OmekAddAlert","Alert_CloseToSide");
```

```
ExternalInterface.call("OmekAddAlert","Alert_OutOfFrame");
ExternalInterface.call("OmekAddAlert","Alert_GoodLocation");
ExternalInterface.call("OmekAddAlert","Alert_CloseToWall");
ExternalInterface.call("OmekAddAlert","Alert_GoodBackground");
ExternalInterface.call("OmekAddAlert","Alert_PlayerEnters");
ExternalInterface.call("OmekAddAlert","Alert_PlayerLeaves");
ExternalInterface.call("OmekAddAlert","Alert_GoodFrameRate");
ExternalInterface.call("OmekAddAlert","Alert_LowFrameRate");
//removing listeners from the sensor to specific alerts
ExternalInterface.call("OmekAddAlert","Alert_GoodLocation");
ExternalInterface.call("OmekRemoveAlert","Alert_GoodFrameRate");
ExternalInterface.call("OmekAddAlert","Alert_CloseToWall");


//ask for the current working directory. return a value to
//ExternalInterface.addCallback("OmekGetWorkingDir", onOmekGetWorkingDir);
ExternalInterface.call("OmekGetWorkingDir","");
//ask for the sensor's properties. return a value to
//ExternalInterface.addCallback("OmekGetSensorProperties", onOmekGetSensorProperties);
ExternalInterface.call("OmekGetSensorProperties","");
//ask for the body dimensions of a specific player. return a value to
//ExternalInterface.addCallback("OmekGetBodyDimensions", onOmekGetBodyDimensions);
ExternalInterface.call("OmekGetBodyDimensions","0");


//get rgb or depth or player mask
ExternalInterface.addCallback("OmekShowImage", onOmekShowImage);
ExternalInterface.addCallback("OmekGetImageResolution", onOmekGetImageResolution);
//ask for the resolution of the rgb image written in the xml. return a value to
//ExternalInterface.addCallback("OmekGetImageResolution", onOmekGetImageResolution);
ExternalInterface.call("OmekGetImageResolution","");

}
```

Modifying the Beckon Flash Example

Now we will add something to this example before moving on to creating our own example. Let's track a new joint: the head.

First off, we need to let Beckon know that we want to receive the head joint in the flash runtime environment. To do this, we need to modify the config.xml file and modify it to match the following code:

```
C:\MyProject\Flash\config.xml
<tracking>
            <skeleton rawSkeleton="true"/>
            <joint name="rightFingerTip" screen="false" smooth="true"/>
            <joint name="leftFingerTip" screen="false" smooth="true"/>
            <joint name="torso" screen="false" smooth="true"/>
            <joint name="head" screen="false" smooth="true"/>
</tracking>
```

Add head tracking into the example by modifying the onOmekJointPosition function that starts on line 164 of the testOmekFlashPlayer.fla file. Following is the new version of the function that you should create:

```
function onOmekJointPosition(jointName:String, playerLabel:String, jointX:String,
jointY:String, jointZ:String, confidence:String):void
{
//give control on mouses to one specific player.
if(playerLabel == "0")
{
if(jointName == "head") {

  myHead.x = stage.stageWidth - Number(jointX) * _screenScaleX + _correctionX;
  myHead.y =Number(jointY) * _screenScaleY + _correctionY;


}
if(jointName == "leftFingerTip")
{
  //mirror X value in order to make the mouse move left and right like the hand.
  leftFingerTip_mc.x = stage.stageWidth - Number(jointX) * _screenScaleX + _correctionX;
  leftFingerTip_mc.y = Number(jointY) * _screenScaleY + _correctionY;

  //debugString_txt.appendText("\nleftFingerTip_mc located at:
("+leftFingerTip_mc.x.toString()+","+leftFingerTip_mc.y.toString()+")");
}
if(jointName == "rightFingerTip")
{
  rightFingerTip_mc.x = stage.stageWidth - Number(jointX) * _screenScaleX + _correctionX;
  rightFingerTip_mc.y = Number(jointY) * _screenScaleY + _correctionY;
}
}
}
```

Finally, export and run OmekBeckonFlash.exe. You should see your movie clip head tracking enabled and working, as shown in Figure 6-5.

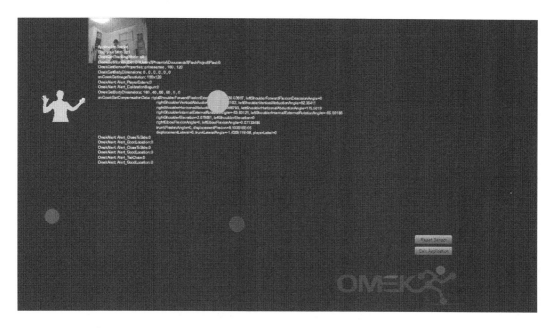

Figure 6-5 *Beckon tracking the added head joint*

Designing A Custom Gesture

Gesture design opens the door to a new world of user experience that's just now being created. When you start designing your gestures, you will want to keep a few basics in mind. Here are seven design strategies to get you started:

1. First, the gesture should feel connected to the activity the user needs to perform. Think about the popular 'pinch to peek' gesture for zooming photos on the iPhone. It feels very intuitive and is an example of excellent gesture design. The motions are natural for making an image larger or smaller, and connect people to their photos in a more organic way.

▩ **Tip** What would be the best gestures for your application or game? Certainly the best would be gestures that require no user manual and very little explanation. Allowing people to try and use your interface with absolutely no prior exposure to your project will immediately let you know if the design is working. Can users figure out your interface naturally, or do they need to stop and ask what to do? Is your interface friendly and inviting enough that users can just start trying it out, or does it feel intimidating? A few false starts can spoil a user's initial reaction to an interface. If the interface continues to behave in unexpected ways, the user will likely quit using it at all.

---

2. A second gesture rule of thumb is to consider user comfort and the body. The days of the body needing to conform to the machine are over. I have continued to wonder why we still use what looks like a glorified typewriter over 100 years later, despite vast leaps in technology. Our QWERTY keyboard does nothing but lead to RSI, Carpel Tunnel, and back pain for thousands of users. Interfaces that are comfortable to use are going to be the most successful for long-term use. Thankfully, with multi touch and computer vision at our disposal for creating user experiences, we no longer need to rely on old paradigms to create interaction models. Simply put, if it hurts, don't do it—and don't ask your customers and users to do it.

3. Third, take into account basic human psychology when designing. Raising your arms up to the sky universally feels uplifting, while kneeling has connotations of prayer and surrender. For example, if you want someone to feel happy while playing your game, it would be wise to read Jane McGonigal's, *Reality is Broken.* She documents many tactics for creating positive emotions in gaming, the most common of which is touching another human. Human touch releases a flood of oxytocin in the brain. Oxytocin is a chemical widely associated with creating happiness in the mind. Gesture based SDKs allow for player interaction, so touch would be a very easy way to trigger positive emotions, bonding, and a feeling of connection in your players.

4. Fourth, use gesture conventions to your advantage and build upon them. There's absolutely no excuse to ignore gestures that people are familiar with from other platforms or interaction models. Take those gestures and make them work for the interface you are designing. At its core, design builds upon existing paradigms and good design advances design discourse.

5. Fifth, don't violate interaction models that users are accustomed to from the real world or other interfaces. Gamers are used to the idea of picking up a sword and they have a specific way they expect to hold and swing it. Take that model into account when designing. Use gestures with arm swings to allow for a fun, more realistic sword fight.

6. Sixth, interaction models should not be in conflict with the world in which they exist. For instance, if a player is carrying a sword on their back in the game, don't make the player go through an interface to access that weapon. Just allow them to reach up and grab it off their back. Otherwise, you will design conflicting, confusing interactions that will be unintuitive to players.

7. Finally, an interface and gestures should work as a whole. Users should be able to easily grasp the gestalt of the UX design and convey it to new users quickly and with ease. Don't change the gesture used for a task to another gesture halfway through the experience. Consider keeping gestures used for similar experiences connected in their design.

In this area, much might be learned from the fields of yoga, neurology, and physical therapy. All three of these fields have extensively explored the mind-body connection. What emotion arises by forms created with the human body? What chemicals are triggered in our brains with which gestures? How will mirror neurons impact group experience design? Without doubt, gestures that you add to your design will have tremendous impact usability.

Adding a New Gesture to the SDK

In Beckon, we can create, edit, and add gestures through GUI interfaces that require no code at all. We are going to create a brand new gesture that doesn't exist in the SDK as of yet and we'll call it from the Flash example. To do this, we need to record ourselves performing the gesture a few times in front of the sensor. To perform a gesture, you pose by putting your body into the form for that gesture. We will pose a few times so that the machine learning environment will have samples to analyze and learn from. Each recording of a pose is considered a sample. Those samples are combined into a Classifier of that gesture. Beckon calls video clips sequences. A sequence is just a recording of a person performing the gesture. Once we are getting good recognition from Beckon, we'll add a listener for this new gesture into Flash. When we perform it, if all goes well, the name of the gesture will appear in the debugString_txt box on the stage to let us know it was recognized. We have to use three tools to go through the complete process:

- The first tool, Omek Beckon Gesture Organizer, lets us add the gesture in name only into the sdk.

- The second application, the Gesture Toolbox, enables us to select the gesture so that we can record Examples. We record examples through the Kinect camera. Record several examples. Once we have a few positive ones, we record a few negative ones as well. From there, we will go into each file and mark each recording, letting Beckon know where the gesture is positively performed by marking it as such. Any unmarked clip or clip area will be analyzed as a negative example.

- Finally, we launch the Gesture Learner, our third application, and tell it where our examples are located. We also tell it a few things about what we are looking for with our gesture. The Gesture Learner will analyze our clips and grade them. Anything less than .96% should send us back into the Gesture Toolbox to get more positive and negative examples. Ideally, we would like a grade of 1.

For the purpose of this chapter's example, I've not included the recording of gestures from different people as test gestures. Ideally, you would record these types of gestures and grade your examples against test examples to make sure you were getting good recognition across many sources. This is an easy step to add and the Beckon SDK has links to a tutorial to guide you through it.

Let's get started. First off, we need to know how Beckon groups gestures into gesture groups it calls classifiers. Again, a classifier is just a set of gesture recording of the exact same gesture that will be analyzed together. These sequences will ultimately describe the classifier for the machine learning environment. We need to go into the Classifier folder in the SDK and add a new folder for our new gesture. Open the folder, which should have the following path:

C:\Beckon SDK\bin\Classifiers

Notice that there are two existing folders, GuiGesturePack and BasicGesturePack. These contain the gestures that come with Beckon. Let's add a folder and call it gameGestures. In that folder, I'd suggest a new folder for each new gesture. For now, let's just make one called leftHandUp. The full path and name should be:

C:\Beckon SDK\bin\Classifiers \gameGestures\leftHandUp

Now create a folder in leftHandUp called examples:

C:\Beckon SDK\bin\Classifiers \gameGestures\leftHandUp\examples

Finally, add one more folder for your output once your gestures are trained:

`C:\Beckon SDK\bin\Classifiers \gameGestures\leftHandUp\output`

Now let's launch one of the three GUI interfaces and add your gesture. Launch the Gesture Organizer, which you'll find at the following location:.

`C:\Beckon SDK\bin\OmekGestgureOrganizer.exe`

Once you have launched the Gesture Organizer, perform the following steps:

1. Click the Add Button and fill in the "Add Gestures" dialog as follows: `Package (gameGestures)`, `File (leftHandUp)`, `Gestures (leftHandUp)`, and `Type` (use "Trained"). For this tutorial, modifying other fields is not necessary.

2. Click the Create Button to add this gesture and its package.

3. Click the Save Button in the Gesture Organizer menu, to apply these changes.

Your gesture now exists in the SDK and an .xml file has been generated. Of course, it doesn't work yet, but it will be available in the tools for marking sequences (Figure 6-6).

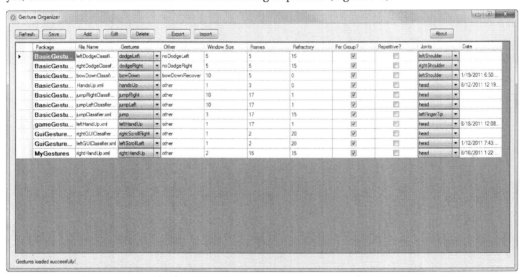

Figure 6-6 *The Gesture Organizer with the added* `leftHandUp` *gesture.*

▓ **Note** For more information about the different options in the Gesture Organizer, please refer to the Gesture Training Manual in the docs folder.

Recording a Gesture

Now that you've added a new gesture, you can record it. Let's open the Gesture Toolbox, which is the application we use to record gestures. The purpose of recording a gesture is to allow Beckon to register the gesture later, when it is performed by a user in front of the sensor.

Execute the Gesture Toolbox by finding and double-clicking the following executable:

```
C:\Beckon SDK\bin\OmekGestgureToolbox.exe
```

There are a few tabs in this application. We will start off with the Recorder tab and then move into the marker tab in the next section.

A word to the wise is that the Gesture Toolbox's interface could be smoother to use. The name of your file is going to be cut off in the viewer. Don't worry; each clip you make will be saved, but you will need to key over to see the name of each clip. Do that by pressing the right-arrow key when a clip's name has focus. You can key over the letters, but there's no way to expand the field.

Clips are in numeric order automatically, but it's easy to forget your place. For this reason, I recommend keeping a list of which clips are positive examples and which are negative examples. It's helpful to know later. A positive example is a video recording of the gesture being performed. A negative example is a recording of a body doing anything but the gesture being trained. These negative examples help describe what the gesture is not. The positive ones tell the machine learning system what the gesture is.

Follow these steps to record some examples of your gesture:

1. In the Recorder tab, select the "examples" folder as the output folder and set the desired number of frames (usually between 200 and 500 frames).

2. Record a sequence of someone performing the desired gesture, by pressing the Record Button. We call this a positive example, since it demonstrates what should be detected as the trained gesture. When performing the gesture by yourself, check the "countdown" option before starting to record. Make sure to move around a bit. You should see dots pop up on each joint. If you don't see dots, you aren't getting joint data.

3. Add more sequences in the same way. Add at least 3 or 4. It's recommended to move around a bit in the pose. Don't just stand stock still. If you do, you'll never see the joints register. Sway slightly, shifting your weight from right to left.

4. Also get a few negative examples of you not doing the gesture. This is very important for successful gesture recognition later when we train our systems.

For the training sequences, try to perform the gesture very clearly, without mixing it with other gestures. With "pose" gestures (like the one in this example), you can stay in the desired pose continuously for most of the sequence, while you modify the style of the pose and its location.

Marking a Gesture

Once you've made several recordings of a gesture, you must tell the SDK which of those recordings represent good versions of the gesture that you want to detect. You do that by marking the places in the recordings where the gesture was performed. These marked clips will be used to train the classifier. Note that it will also analyze sections not marked, considering those as negative examples, so be careful to select all frames where the gesture is performed correctly.

Here is the process to follow in marking a gesture:

1. Go to the Marker Tab and open the video sequence that you have recorded. The video sequence will be loaded and displayed in the middle window.

2. Let the clip run and make sure that the gesture is performed as expected, and that the tracking of the player is correct. If there is a problem, either delete the clip and record a new one, or use the "Skip In/Out" options to ignore the problematic frames.

3. Select the gesture to be marked in the gestures list at the top left window. In this example, the gesture is called leftHandUp and it is located in the gameGestures package. Select it by expanding the package and clicking the gesture name.

4. View the video sequence and mark the gesture using the Mark In and Mark Out buttons.

5. Repeat these steps for all the video sequences you have recorded with positive examples

For your negative examples, load your clip, make sure you have the gesture selected, and save it. Notice in Figure 6-7 the highlighted button after the sequence name with an ellipsis, or three dots, as the label. This button with no name and only dots is the button that allows you to open your file viewer. If you go into the folder where you are saving your gestures, you will see a list of clips by number. Remember that I mentioned to keep track of which performances were the negative examples? Now that you need to load the sequence video clips, it's really helpful to know which ones are negative examples. Select a negative example and it will open. You can press the regular video controls to play the clip and mark the negative sequence using the exact same series of steps you used to mark the positive sequence.

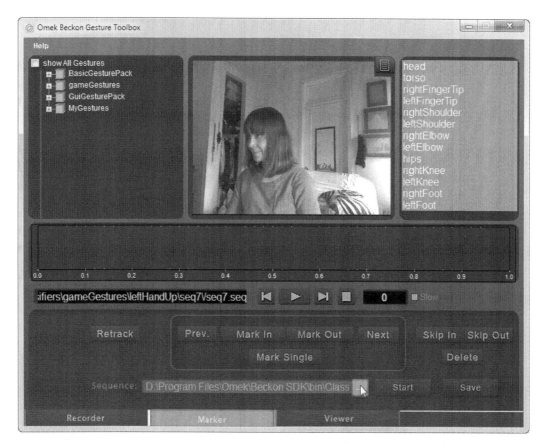

Figure 6-7.*Omek Beckon Gesture Toolbox with the Sequence open button selected.*

Training a Gesture

After recording and marking comes the training stage. In this stage, you will train the gesture based on the recorded video sequences, using the Gesture Learner tool. Here you will find out if you did a good job of performing the gesture in the clips or if you will need to go back and repeat the process.

Begin by opening and executing the GestureLearner. Double-click the following executable:

```
C:\Beckon SDK\bin\Omek Beckon Gesture Learner.exe
```

Then follow these steps:

1. Go to the Files Tab and add the trainings sequences. Click the Add Directory Button, select the "examples" folder, and click the OK Button. This will add all of the contained sequences.

▪ **Tip** If you saved sequences of the target gesture in other folders, you can repeat the previous step and add them as well.

---

2. Now set the "Output Files" options. Select your "output" folder created earlier. It will contain all of the outputs of the training process. Click the OK Button.

3. Ensure that the "Package" field shows the name of your new package (gameGestures).

4. Verify that the "Classifier" field holds the name of the file that you entered in the Gesture Organizer. That file name should be leftHandUp.xml.

5. Go to the Gesture Tab and set the "Per Gesture Configuration" options. Click on the "Gesture" field and select the target gesture (leftHandUp). Press the Add Button to insert this gesture into the "Active Gestures" list.

You have now selected the gesture that will be trained. Sometimes you may want to train more than one gesture in a single process; in these cases, you will repeat steps 1-5, adding required gestures one after the other.

The tab contains all of the parameters that can be modified for the training process. It is beyond the scope of this tutorial to explain all of these. We will examine a few examples only, while the rest can be learned from the Gesture Manual document. The parameters are divided into different groups. In every group, you can see a check box called "Auto". Checking this option will indicate that the Learner should find the parameters automatically.

Set the Advanced Tab parameters as follows:

Gesture Type. In our example, the trained gesture is a pose and not a motion, so we will check the "Pose" option. Gestures like jump or punch will be a "Moving" gesture. Leave the "Auto" option checked.

Data Processing. Leave the "Auto" option selected.

Joints. First, use the default values ("Auto" and "Both") selected. Later on, you can change these values and see how they influence the results. "Upper" will use only the upper-body for the training, while "Lower" will use the lower-body only. Selecting "Both" will try all of the body joints.

Learning Method. Select "Fast" for the first time; this will train the gesture faster, so you can readily see some results. Later on, try to change this value to "Best" to see its influence. The "Fast" and the "Best" methods use different options, so the results may be different between the two methods.

After setting all of the wanted parameters, it's time to run the training process. You do that as follows:

1. Click the Add Button, at the bottom part of the window, to add a training job with the current values. Note that the training process will not execute until you click the Run Button in the next step

2. Click the Run Button to run all the jobs in the list. The jobs will run sequentially (one after the other), and their results will be displayed immediately as every job finishes.

3. If a job ends successfully, a "success" icon (a check shape) is displayed and the score of this classifier is shown in the list. A "failure" icon will be displayed in case of an error ("X" shaped).

4. Double click the line with the job name to see more details about the score.

You can run many training jobs at the same time, and you can add more as the current jobs are running. Simply go back to the previous tabs (Files, Gesture, and Advanced), change any parameter, and add a new job. Note that since randomness is applied to the algorithm, running the same parameters twice may not result in the same output! Please refer to the Gesture Training Manual for more details about the training options.

■ **Note** f you have closed the Learner and want to retrieve the parameters of an old job, simply click the "Load" button in the "Files" tab, browse to the folder where your required output is saved, and select the XML file.

Testing a Gesture

A classifier is created and published for every gesture that you create using the method described so far. It is the classifier that enables you to use a gesture from Flash. Publishing a classifier simply refers to adding it into the SDK, just as we did for leftHandUp.

Having published a classifier, you may want to test the classifier with a live camera. Here is how to run a test:

1. Open the Gesture Toolbox and go to the Viewer tab.

2. Select the Input source (in the bottom right part of the screen):

   • For live testing with a camera, select the Sensor option. Then select the type of camera from the menu below.

   • For a sequence, select the Sequence option. Then browse for the sequence, or type its path in the text-box below.

3. Press the Start Button to initiate the execution of the tracking.

Select the target gestures in the Gestures Display (top left part of the screen). You may choose more than one gesture. Perform the gesture. If you did everything correctly, you should see your gesture register. See figure 6.8 for an example of the leftHandUp gesture correctly tracking

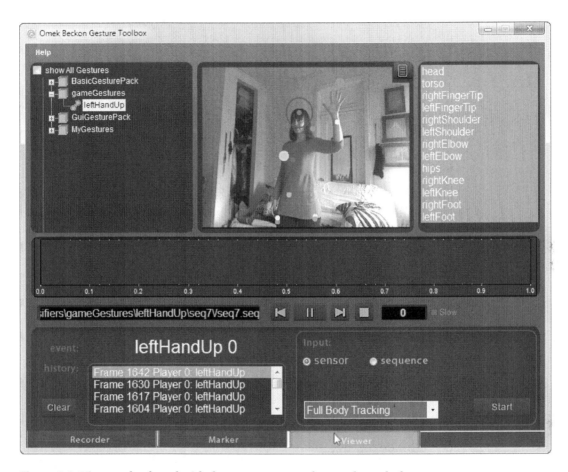

Figure 6-8. *Viewer tab selected with the gesture open and correctly tracked.*

Adding a Gesture for use by Flash

Now we can add our new gesture into our Flash file's Actionscript. The first step is to add the gesture listener into our calls. Find the following code block and add the bold lines into your code:

```
//adding listeners for the sensor to specific gestures (see documentation for full list of
  gestures available)
ExternalInterface.call("OmekAddGesture","leftPush");
ExternalInterface.call("OmekAddGesture","rightClick");
ExternalInterface.call("OmekAddGesture","jumpNoHands");
ExternalInterface.call("OmekAddGesture","leftHandUp");

//removing listeners from the sensor to specific gestures
ExternalInterface.call("OmekRemoveGesture","leftPush");
```

```
ExternalInterface.call("OmekRemoveGesture","rightClick");
ExternalInterface.call("OmekRemoveGesture","jumpNoHands");
ExternalInterface.call("OmekRemoveGesture","leftHandUp");
```

Save and export the application. Then launch OmekBeckonFlash.exe. Now, when we perform the leftHandUp gesture, the debugString_txt box should output the gesture's name. The box should pop up and read "leftHandUp." If you are not seeing that result, go back and carefully check that you've performed each step in this chapter correctly.

Building Functionality Based on a Gesture

Now that our new gesture is working and is being recognized, we can use the gesture to trigger functionality in the application. Let's go back into our code block add some new functionality to draw a yellow box near our left fingertip when the application registers the gesture as having been performed. Add the below code into the testOmekFlashPlayer.fla file above the function OnOmekGesture(). This code just allows us to draw a yellow square graphic onscreen at every point where the application correctly tracks the new leftHandUp gesture. In figure 6.9, you will see the gesture tracked at the moment my left arm got to a certain point on screen above my shoulder.

```
var gestureSeen:MovieClip = new MovieClip();
var xNum:Number = 80;
var yNum:Number = 80;
gestureSeen.graphics.beginFill(0xFFcc00);
gestureSeen.graphics.drawRect(xNum, yNum, 30,30);

function onOmekGesture(gestureName:String, playerLabel:String):void

{

        if (gestureName == "leftHandUp") {
        stage.addChild(gestureSeen);
        gestureSeen.x = xNum;
        gestureSeen.y = yNum;


        }
}
```

Add two more lines of code to get the position of your left finger tip and assign it to the xNum and yNum variables. The two lines are shown in bold in the following example. Find the same block of code in the example file and add the two lines shown in bold.

```
function onOmekJointPosition(jointName:String, playerLabel:String, jointX:String,
jointY:String, jointZ:String, confidence:String):void
{
  //give control on mouses to one specific player.
  if(playerLabel == "0")
  {

  }
  if(jointName == "leftFingerTip")
```

```
{
    //mirror X value in order to make the mouse move left and right like  the hand.
    leftFingerTip_mc.x = stage.stageWidth - Number(jointX) *_screenScaleX + _correctionX;
    leftFingerTip_mc.y = Number(jointY) * _screenScaleY + _correctionY;
    xNum = leftFingerTip_mc.x;
    yNum = leftFingerTip_mc.y;
}
```

Save and export the example project. Run the example again. Perform the LeftHandUp gesture. You should see that Beckon will place a box on the screen at the position of your fingertip at the time you performed the gesture (Figure 6-9).

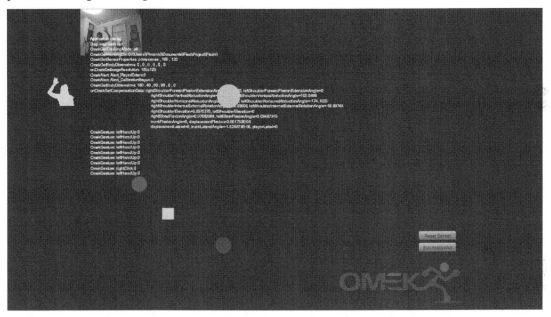

Figure 6-9. *Beckon registering the leftHandUp gesture and moving a box to the location of my left finger tip where on screen the gesture was performed.*

I hope that this example has introduced you to the main ideas behind the Beckon SDK. First, we went over what Beckon does and then we got it up and running. We then added in new tracking functionality to the existing example for your head. From there, it's easy to map graphics to a skeleton. Next, we went over some basics of interface design. Then we created our own gesture and added it to the Beckon SDK and successful added a listener for it in Flash. Finally, we added a graphic to indicate when—and, more importantly, where—our gesture occurred. That should give you enough of a start with Beckon to create a basic interface.

CHAPTER 7

3D Games and User Interfaces with Unity

For this chapter, we are going to be using a very popular game engine called Unity. By integrating OpenNI, NITE, and Sensor Kinect in Unity, we will control a 3D character and multiple user interfaces. After we cover the main components, we will build an example of each from the bottom up.

A game engine is a system designed for creating and developing video games, installation spaces, and interfaces. What you can do with a game engine goes far beyond just creating games. Unity is used commonly to create architectural installations and 3D user interfaces. Game engines are designed to work with mobile devices, computers, and game consoles. Most offer a rendering engine for 2D and 3D graphics, a physics engine (for collision detection and adding physics), sound, scripting, animation, and more. A game engine is a real-time 3D environment easily repurposed in many ways. It can create brilliant responsive environments, 3D projection maps, and interactive displays just as easily as it can create games.

So what is a game engine exactly? It's a game creation tool, which is different from a 3D package. You usually would not use an engine to model your 3D characters but to put them together and turn them into a playable game. Three-dimensional software packages at every level of the industry export files that engines support. If you are new to 3D and want to try it out for free, check out Blender and Google SketchUp. For more serious users, you are already most likely using Maya or 3D Studio Max. If you are a student, Maya also has a free educational version. Note that .fbx files are native for Unity support, and Unity converts all polygons to polygon triangles.

Unity is a great game platform that's competitive with much more expensive engines, such as the Unreal Engine, but it has a free edition. If a game or application created in Unity grosses more than $100,000, Unity requires a license be purchased. This makes the free edition ideal for beginners. This edition limits the complexity of the games and disables some of the pro features such as mobile functionality, but you can still make a good game with the tools available.

The Kinect galvanized the open source community After the Kinect data stream was successfully converted into useable data by the Open Kinect community, the indie development scene exploded with activity. Games, art installations, and other experimental computer user interactions were created all over the world.

Installing Unity and Supporting Software

Let's get started. First, download Unity from `http://unity3d.com/`. Install Unity as you would install any other application on your platform. I will be using Mac OS X 10.6.8 for the examples here, but Unity is platform agnostic as are the ZigFu scripts we will be running.

▓ **Note** This chapter is created with Unity version 3.4. Older versions are not compliant with the software covered here.

Next, we are going to use an extremely easy install script from ZigFu. ZigFu has created a package with one install script that includes OpenNI, Sensor Kinect, and NITE. ZigFu has the unique attribute of being written by two ex-PrimeSense employees and two other developers. PrimeSense was the company that created NITE. As a result, these Unity scripts for OpenNI are the most stable available and have the advantage of being open source. ZigFu is Amir Hirsch, Ted Blackman, Roee Shenberg, and Shlomo Zippel. When asked where they got their name from, they cited the '90s meme, All Your Base Are Belong to Us. In addition, they think of moving in front of a Kinect as "zigging."

Download the Installer script from `www.Zigfu.com`. In addition, download the Unity package on `www.Zigfu.com`. This is the package we will import to run Kinect in Unity. Unzip these files and move them into your Documents folder.

▓ **Caution** ZigFu recommends a complete deinstall of Open Kinect, NITE, and OpenNI before running their install.sh script. I found deinstalling unnecessary, but you may want to follow ZigFu's recommendation.

Following are the steps for executing ZigFu's installer script on a Mac. The process on a Windows PC will be similar, and perhaps even easier, as the Windows installer enables you do everything with a single click.

1. Launch a terminal window. Do that on the Mac by going to Mac ➤ Application ➤ Utilities ➤ Terminal.

A terminal window should open, and you should see something like that in Figure 7-1.

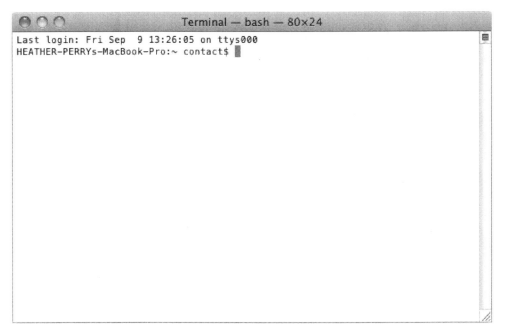

Figure 7-1. The Mac OS X terminal window

2. Navigate to the folder containing the installer script that you downloaded. For example, I issued the following command on my system:

```
cd  Documents/ZigFuOpenNIMac
```

3. Issue the following command to execute the installer script as the root user:

```
sudo sh install.sh
```

4. The sudo command might be new to you. There's a user in your Mac OS that's a superuser, or root user, used for system administration. This user account has privileges that your regular account does not have. The sudo command allows you to execute a single command as if you were logged on as this special user known as root.

5. You will be prompted for your user password. Enter it. The installation will run, and the following lines of code will appear in the Terminal window.

```
You Know What You Doing (Installing OpenNI)
Installing OpenNI
***************************
copying shared libraries...OK
copying executables...OK
copying include files...OK
...
*** DONE ***
For Great Justice... (Type "sh test.sh" to run the UserTracker demo)
```

6. Now we are going to test to make sure everything installed correctly by running the test script. Type the following command and press Enter:

```
sh test.sh
```

7. This window should pop open, and you should see yourself moving around, as shown in Figure 7-2. What you see in the figure is a depth map. A depth map is an image channel that contains information relating to the distance to the surfaces of scene objects from a viewpoint, in this case from the Kinect.

The installation is complete! You are ready to move on and explore what Unity has to offer. Make sure to close the PrimeSense User Tracker Viewer before moving on to avoid conflicts with subsequent examples.

Figure 7-2. A Kinect depth map as generated by Unity

Exploring the Unity Interface

Launch Unity. Let's create a project and explore the interface together.

Projects

Here's how to create a project:

1. Select File ➤ New Project from the menu.

2. It's a good idea to always import Unity's Standard Assets. In the popup, you
    will see a whole list of possibilities to include in your project. Select Standard
    Assets and press Create Project.

3. Import the ZigFu Unity package for all of the examples. Start by selecting
    Assets ➤ Import Package ➤ Custom Package from the menu.

4. Navigate to your Documents folder and import the following file:

UnityOpenNIBindings-v1.1.unitypackage

5. From the ensuing popup, just let Unity import all the appropriate libraries for
    the project it needs.

Unity should now have a few tabs open. The first thing you are going to want to do is note that in the
upper left you see two tabs, Scene and Game. Click Game to switch to the Game tab.

The Workspace

To make working in Unity easier, grab the Game tab and drag it to the left. It will pop in as its own
separate tab area. The gray bar between the two windows can be adjusted by dragging. After moving the
tab, you should see results similar to those in Figure 7-3.

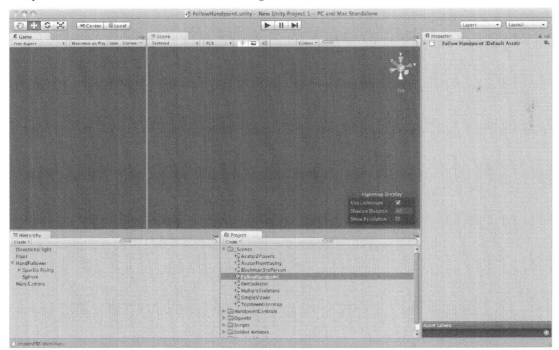

Figure 7-3. The Unity workspace

The left tab is now Game Viewer. In this tab, you can see everything that is in the current scene in 3D space from the perspective of the camera. A camera in 3D space works just like a regular camera and should be positioned to frame all the appropriate visual elements in the scene.

The tab on the right of the Game Viewer is the Scene Viewer tab. This tab shows the 3D world of the selected scene. You can think of scenes exactly like you'd think of levels. For each level in your game, you'll create a scene. In the upper-right corner of the Scene Viewer, there is an exotic creature found in many 3D packages known as a Gizmo, and yes, that's the official name. Fear not, it will not reproduce if you feed it after midnight or get it wet. It shows you the X, Y, Z, and perspective views. It's easy to remember X, Y, and Z as R, G, and B in this color scene. Click and rotate on the X, Y, Z, or center cube (perspective view) axis to see the game from these angles.

▨ **Note** Viewing from different angles doesn't move the camera, only what the user is looking at in the current scene.

The final tab to the far right is the Inspector. If you know Flash, you can think of this tab like the Properties Inspector. The Inspector allows you to set the properties for a selected object's components. The Inspector also allows you to attach scripts to game objects to introduce functionality in Unity. This is exactly what ZigFu has already done to make their examples work. ZigFu designed a basic scene with game objects and then attached scripts to the game objects to bind with OpenNI.

You'll see two tabs on the bottom of the workspace. The bottom left tab is your Hierarchy Viewer. Everything in this tab is actually an object in your game. The bottom right tab is the Project folder for the current project. Everything in this folder is hiding in User ➤ New Unity Project 1 ➤ Assets. Anything added to the Assets file will automatically update in this tab viewer. However, the object will not be in the game until it is added to a scene by dragging it into the Scene or Inspector.

Basic Navigation and Transform Tools

Now let's run down the buttons surrounding the tabs. The buttons to your top left (Figure 7-4) are your basic navigation and transform tools with key commands that match most 3D applications.

Figure 7-4. Basic navigation and transform tools

The buttons in Figure 7-4 operate as follows, working from left to right. The letters in parentheses are the keyboard shortcuts.

- The Hand tool (Q) allows you to move around the 3D world.

- The Move tool (W) allows you to move around a selected game object in the Scene tab.

- The Rotate tool (W) allows you to rotate around your selected game object in the Scene tab.

- The Scale tool (R) allows you to scale a selected game object in the Scene tab.

Another handy key command to know is F. Pressing F on your keyboard will focus the Scene tab on any game object selected in the Hierarchy tab.

Play Controls

The next buttons to the right are the play controls (Figure 7-5).

Figure 7-5. *Unity's play controls*

The Play button runs the current scene. If you press the Play button while the scene is playing, the scene stops. Unity has a specific interface particularity to be aware of. If in Play mode, these buttons will glow blue. Any changes made in the Inspector during this time to game object properties will be lost when the scene is stopped. There is no way to save changes made during Play mode unless you add an additional plug-in to Unity. If you hit on a property change that you like while in Play mode, write that change down and reenter it once you are out of Play mode.

▪ **Tip** A three-button mouse is critical for working in Unity's 3D space. All three buttons are used to smoothly move around the scene in 3D space. Holding down Option and left-clicking allows you to pan the perspective. The middle mouse scroll zooms in and out of a scene. Pressing the scroll middle button down will toggle into the Hand tool. Right-clicking rotates perspective. Option+right-clicking provides an additional Zoom tool.

Understanding ZigFu's Relation to Unity

ZigFu is a set of C# scripts that bind with OpenNI and PrimeSense's NITE to allow Unity to access NITE's functionality. OpenNI is an open source standard for creating compatibility across the newly emerging field of natural interaction devices, applications, and middleware. OpenNI is an abstraction layer that integrates middleware with hardware and applications.

OpenNI and NITE

OpenNI has been geared mainly toward 3D sensors, but nothing in OpenNI is specific to PrimeSense's NITE or the Kinect. OpenNI is an interface that allows developers of middleware such as NITE get a depth stream, skeleton data, audio, infrared (IR), hand points, an RGB image, and gesture detection. OpenNI doesn't specifically care how these points were generated or from where.

OpenNI relies upon modules to retrieve device data and pass that data into OpenNI and any middleware. Anyone can write a module for any camera or sensor and register it with OpenNI. NITE is middleware that gives digital devices the power to translate and respond to user interaction without wearable equipment or controls.

■ **Note** The important point to understand about OpenNI is that is it not specific to hardware or middleware. OpenNI can be used with any OpenNI-compliant hardware. For example, you can use OpenNI with the PrimeSense reference design, the Microsoft Kinect, the Asus Xtion, and with any OpenNI-compliant middleware such as NITE, and soon Beckon.

NITE, then, is the intermediary standing between OpenNI and your application, in this case Unity. In the case of the Kinect, PrimeSense made not only the middleware but also the motion sensor chip inside the Kinect. This really changes nothing practically, but it's a fun fact to know and part of what makes NITE so robust.

Unity and ZigFu

Unity allows users to create scripts and attach those scripts to game objects as components. Components are how game functionality is added to any game, and they drive the game objects. ZigFu has created scripts for Unity to bind, or talk with, OpenNI.

ZigFu has created sample scripts to familiarize users with OpenNI's functionality. Before ZigFu, developers in Unity wrote their own bindings. There's still nothing stopping developers from doing this now should they be so inclined and skilled. With the way Unity works, you can very easily attach the ZigFu scripts onto one object and any custom scripts that you might create onto that same object or any other object.

Unity is surprisingly tolerant of this kind of development. In fact, Unity supports not one but *three* scripting languages: JavaScript, C#, and Boo. Developers can use all three simultaneously, and there's no need to choose one language over the other. One of your game object's components can be in C# and the other in Boo.

Running the ZigFu Game Examples

Go to your Project folder and open the folder called _Scenes. These are the ZigFu-created scenes, which are examples demonstrating OpenNI functionality. Some of these you need two people to actually use, so be prepared to get a friend to help at some point to run the multiplayer examples.

ZigFu divides examples into two categories: game and interface. We'll go over the game examples first, in this section, and then the interface examples.

Avatar2Players

Double-click Avatar2Players (two people required). You should see two soldiers standing side by side on a floor, as shown in Figure 7-6. If you cannot see them in your Scene tab, adjust the view until you do see them. You can select a soldier in your Hierarchy tab and press F on your keyboard. Scene view will now focus on the selected object.

Figure 7-6. *The Avatar2Players game*

OpenNI is not tracking a player yet. That's because you need to play each scene to start the tracking. Press the black Play button now.

You will now see a little yellow view port in the bottom of your Game tab. Make sure that you and your fellow player are both visible in the camera view. You both need to stand in the calibration pose to calibrate OpenNI. This pose is exactly like the stick 'em up pose in a bank robbery. Both hands up now, please!

Make sure your elbows are parallel to your shoulders and your hands are at the same height. After the Kinect catches you and your partner as the players, you will see the 3D model jump into your body positions.

■ **Note** OpenNI is removing the calibration pose by the end of 2011. If you are reading this chapter after then, you might not need to do a calibration pose. Dance around and see if you are tracked. If you are, then good. If not, then try the calibration pose.

Let's now look a little bit deeper into this scene from Figure 7-6 and how to navigate around it. Do the following:

1. Click Soldier in the Hierarchy tab.

2. Direct your attention to the right Inspector tab.

3. Turn down the arrow next to OpenNI Skeleton (script).

Now visible is a list of all the joints you can get access to with OpenNI and what game objects the joints are attached to in Unity. Note how all the corresponding joints are mapped onto the game objects. The script joints coming from OpenNI are on the left, and the game objects in the scene are listed on the right. They have simply been named to match the names of the joint they correspond to. Single-click any game object joint on the right of the list, and you will see it jump to its associated object listed in the Hierarchy tab. Double-clicking will open that object up in the Inspector. To go back to the Soldier, simply single-click it in the Hierarchy again.

In the Hierarchy tab, you will see all objects in the game. In this example, there is a Directional Light, which is lighting the scene. Next down in the list is the Floor. Click it to see the components attached to this game object. The Transform component is on every game object. Next, you will see the Box Collider, Mesh Renderer with the shaders for the Soldier, and the floor and their respective Normalmap. A Mesh Renderer takes the geometry from the Mesh Filter and renders it at the location defined by an object's Transform component in the Inspector. A normal map, or normal mapping, is a way to make an object look like it has a higher polygonal count than it actually does by faking lighting and dents via a 2D file that's applied to the mesh of an object. Creating normals, meshes, and textures is beyond the scope of this tutorial, but is part of every 3D workflow. See the manual for your 3D package to learn more.

The next object in the Hierarchy tab is the Main Camera. Open this object and note that there is a ZigFu script applied to it called ExitOnEscape that allows you to exit a game when you press Escape. You can add this script to any scene where you want this behavior. The script is specific just to this ZigFu example and not part of OpenNI.

■ **Note** To add a script component to a game object, select the game object in the Hierarchy tab to open up the object's list of components in the Inspector. This is a very straightforward process, but it feels strange the first time you do it. All you are doing is attaching a new component, a script component, to your game object via dragging it into the Inspector Window with that game object's components revealed. You expose an object's components whenever you select it in the Hierarchy tab. If you need help, there are several tutorial videos on YouTube. In addition, visit the Unity forums at www.unity3d.com. The Unity community provides good support; the user forums are full of programmers who are kind enough to help newbies out. If you ever get stuck in a jam, the forums should be the first place you turn to for help.

Following are some of the scripts that you can add to a game object:

ChangeColor is for changing the color of the boxes in the ItemSelector scene.

Exitonescape exits the game when Escape is pressed.

ObjectPeruser simply instantiates a Prefab for every detected user and is used in the TopDownUserMap scene.

StartSessesionMessage displays the "perform focus gesture to start session" when you are not in a session.

The next object is the sensor object. Select this object and notice that in the Inspector tab several OpenNI scripts are attached. The sensor object itself is an empty game object. Unity allows you to create empty game objects. This empty object was created to attach scripts to it that run in the scene. These scripts are all related to OpenNI functionality, and are as follows:

Open NIUser Tracker: Allows for Unity to track users up to the maximum number of users OpenNI registers. There is no default maximum number.

Open NIDepthMapViewer: Simply displays the Kinect depth map in your game when it is running. Remember it will not be visible until the game is running.

OpenNIUsers Radar: Pops a dark gray user tracker box up on-screen in the game with a number attached to each specific user the game registers. If you want to use this script in a newly created scene, you must link this script to the Open NIUser Tracker in the Inspector.

Open NISplit Screen Skeleton Control: Allows users to have two players on-screen at once. This might be helpful for a first-person shooter with a split screen.

The final object in the Hierarchy is the Soldier. Soldier is a Prefab; that's why it is blue. A Prefab is a collection of game objects and components that can be used again and again in a game. They are saved in the Project tab view. Prefabs are basic functionality in Unity.

Soldier is actually a ZigFu-created Prefab you can add to any scene. Look in the Project tab and open the OpenNI folder and then the Prefabs. The Prefab Soldier is located within. To add a Prefab to a scene, simply drag the Prefab from the Project folder in the Scene Viewer.

AvatarFrontFacing

AvatarFrontFacing is almost exactly like Avatar2Players, but it has just one Skeleton, and it implements some additional functionality. Double-click AvatarFrontFacing and play the scene. Do the Calibration pose and watch yourself dance around as a soldier.

Select your Sensor Game Object in the Hierarchy tab. Notice the last script component added, OpenNIContext. The OpenNIContext script allows .oni files to be loaded instead of using the live sensor. (.oni files are files that contain prerecorded skeleton data.) To record .oni files, use NIViewer, which comes with OpenNI. (There's more documentation on recording .oni files in the OpenNI manual.) Any .oni file you recorded can easily be linked in Unity using the OpenNIContext component. This is an easy way to do very cheap and effective motion capture without a motion capture suite.

TopDownUserMap

TopDownUserMap shows a top-down game map in which the Kinect drives the location of the player on the floor. The UsersContainer Object in the Hierarchy tab has the Object Per Use and the Open NIUser Tracker scripts attached to it.

Blockman3rdPerson

Blockman3rdPerson adds a few new bits of functionality. Run it and watch what happens. The skeleton is made from Unity game objects, and the camera follows the Blockman in space.

Let's look at the Hierarchy tab to see what is in this example. First, there's a Blockman Container. Open it to find the Blockman Prefab. This is another ZigFu Prefab you can use in any of your projects.

Click the Blockman to open it in the Inspector. Note something new: after the list of joints, notice there are three check boxes again. This time, unlike with the Soldiers Prefab, Update Joint Positions is checked. Uncheck that option and run the example again. See the difference? The game objects no longer change rotation as you move. In fact, the whole skeleton is now wrong. Recheck the option to put things right again and move forward.

Next, look at the Camera settings. Select the Camera in the Hierarchy tab, and in the Inspector, notice the new script Smooth Follow. Smooth Follow is a default Unity script that can be found in the Standard Assets folder we imported in the beginning of our project. In the Project tab, open the Standard Assets folder and then the Scripts subfolder. Smooth Follow is here, and it can be dropped onto any camera and told what game object to follow. Here the script causes the camera to follow the Blockman's Head.

Sensor sits at the bottom of our Hierarchy tab again and looks very similar to previous examples. It's an empty game object with the OpenNI scripts attached. Here we are using the Open NISingle Skeleton Controller just as we were in the AvatarFrontFacing example.

Running the Interface Examples

Moving forward, we are now going to look at the next examples used to create user experiences. Open and play FollowHandPoint in the _Scenes folder in our Project Tab. Try it out. Sparkly right? You'll see Unity's default Ellipsoid Particle Emitter component playing in the background while the OpenNI script tracks a sphere.

All that's happening here is that the Follow Hand Point (script) is attached to the Hand Follower Object in the Hierarchy. The script exists inside the Project tab in the Scripts subfolder HandpointControls. Open and note it. We will use it later to build an example from scratch.

Inside Hand Follower in the Hierarchy tab is the parent game object holding two other game objects we haven't covered yet, particle systems. A particle system is a system of fuzzy particles. They are frequently used to generate stars, fire, and other natural phenomena. These systems can be used and abused in interesting ways. Although particle systems are outside the scope of this chapter, they are worth a future look. Create them just like any other game object, by choosing the following menu option:

Main Menu ➤ Game Object ➤ Create Other ➤ Particle System

■ **Note** The following scenes are more complex and perhaps not ideal for beginners; however, anyone can run them and play them. In addition, beginners are welcome to modify examples to their own ends until they have a better understanding of Unity. These scenes are here for more advanced users interested in creating interfaces.

Item Selector

The subsequent example in the _Scenes folder is Item Selector. Open and play this scene now. This example features new functionality for interface design. In the Hierarchy tab, there are six objects: one camera, four planes, and an empty game object called Static Menu. All of the OpenNI scripts are attached here. Select Static Menu and notice the scripts in the Inspector.

Item Selector Scripts

The Static Menu game object has all of the scripts for this scene attached to it. Select Static Menu to expose its components in the Hierarchy tab. Expand the Items arrow of the Static Menu script. This script can take as many game objects as needed. Simply drag game objects onto the elements you want the game objects attached to. Element 0 has Plane 1 and so forth.

▒ **Note** The Static Menu script is a complex composite hand point control that reacts to the lower-level events from the building blocks ZigFu provides. To open a script and look at what is made of, right-click while over it in the Inspector and choose Edit Script or click the gear icon in the far right corner of the script name.

The check box Select on Push is our first gesture. Push simply is a quick push forward with your hand in space. There's not much to it really. Try performing it a few times while the scene is playing to get the feel for it. When you perform it successfully over one of the planes, the box will turn from green (highlighted) to blue (selected).

The next script component attached to this game object is Push Detector. Push Detector is another one of ZigFu's custom scripts that is not part of OpenNI. For those out there with more programming experience, you can write your own detector using the ZigFu primitives such as:

```
Hand_Create(Vector3 position)
Hand_Update(Vector3 position)
Hand_Destroy()
PushDetector_Push()
PushDetector_Release()
PushDetector_Click()
ItemSelector_Select(int index)
ItemSelector_Next()
ItemSelector_Prev()
```

Fader, another custom ZigFu script, maps a physical region in space to a normalized 0-1 range. The Item Selector can then take the 0-1 range and split it into logical regions with hysteresis between them, including special scroll regions.

When the Item Selector scene is running, there are two faders because the Push Detector implicitly adds one in runtime. The Push Detector fader is on the Z axis, and the other fader is the X axis. The size represents physical size (in millimeters), so 300 is 30 cm, or about 1 ft.

Item Selector Parameters

Some of the Item Selector parameters are as follows:

Number of items: How many logical items the script detects.

Hysteresis: A value between 0 and 1. It defines overlap between logical items, prevents the selected index from "bouncing" between two logical areas. Different applications need different settings, and they can be tweaked in development.

Scroll Region: How much of the range is dedicated to a scroll region. For example, 0.2 would be 20% from each side dedicated to scrolling (sending the Next and Prev messages).

Item Selector Operation

To fully understand what the Item Selector does, create a blank game object and drag a fader and item selector into the object. In addition, add a new script that listens to the Item Selector messages and prints them out. Let's create a script to output which items are selected to the console. To create a script, go to Main Menu ➤ Assets ➤ Create ➤ C#script. Name your script in your project. Select the script in the Hierarchy and choose Open. This will open Unity's scripting environment. Type in the following code:

```
void ItemSelector_Select(int index)
{
  print("Item selector select " + index);
}

void ItemSelector_Next()
{
  print("Item selector next");
}

void ItemSelector_Prev()
{
  print("Item selector prev");
}
```

Now add the script to the game object you created. In addition, you are going to need to manually link up the Fader to the Item Selector in the Inspector. This will print the element you are focused on in the console. To view the console, press Shift+Com+C or go to Main Menu ➤ Window ➤ Console.

The various wait times control the repeat logic of the scrolling (similar to holding down on a keyboard key: you get the first keypress, slight pause, and then repeated keypressing slowly accelerating). The Session Manager waits for the focus gesture and starts a hand point session. The Session Manager heads up the display on the left of the screen seen only in Plat mode is added implicitly, such as OpenNIContext, but can also be added explicitly if you want to change the default settings (which gestures to listen to, for example).

The OpenNISessionManager provides a wrapper for the HandTracking and GestureDetection OpenNI streams. The main advantage of this model is that the gesture detector is based on a raw depth stream; no skeleton detector needed. This means that ZigFu's hand tracker will work even when you are on the couch covered with a blanket and do not resemble any humanoid form. Just do the gesture and you're in control!

CoverFlow

CoverFlow creates your basic carousel user experience. The Menu Game Object has a hand point controller, fader, scrolling menu, and dummy feed. The scrolling menu adds just that to your scene. You can set direction, window size, dampening, and scroll region size. The main difference between a static and scrolling menu is that the scrolling menu is going to be the actual parent of all children added to it.

Here are the main properties of the Scrolling Menu component in more detail:

Direction: Distance between menu items

RepositionBasedOnBounds: Should the menu layout items be based on their actual bounds, or just based on the "Direction" property?

WindowSize: How many on-screen items before scrolling. Passed to ItemSelector

ScrollRegionSize: Passed to ItemSelector

The dummy feed just generates dummy meshes and is a custom ZigFu script. You can change mesh color and other features after selecting the Menu Item component that's linked to this script in the Hierarchy tab.

Slide Viewer

Slide Viewer is a basic slide viewer that is very similar in nature to CoverFlow. However, the feed isn't a dummy feed, but a feed of images for a folder. Path is where you set the path to these images, and your search pattern is for the type of files you want it to include from this directory.

Creating a Skeleton from Scratch

Unity and OpenNI are a powerful combination. With them, you can create a skeleton from scratch. The following steps walk you through the process. A skeleton is a term associated with a visualization of all possible joints an API can detect. In this case, we will make a "stick man skeleton." The reason you'd be interested in doing this is to see that your tracking is working and to later to replace your default game objects with real graphics created in a program like Maya. Bones, rigging, and character animation are beyond the scope of this tutorial, but all 3D packages have plenty of documentation about how to do this. In addition, see the Unity manual for instructions specific to Unity.

Task 1. Add the OpenNI Functionality

Your first step is to create a new scene and add some OpenNI functionality. Here is the process to follow:

1. Go to the Main Menu. Choose File ➤ New Scene.

2. Save your scene as MySkeleton.

3. In that new scene, create an empty game object and add the OpenNI scripts onto it. Choose Main Menu ➤ Game Object ➤ Create Empty to create a new game object.

4. Rename the game object OpenNI Functionality. Do that by pressing Ctr+right-click and choosing the Rename option. Note: You can actually specify any name that you like. For example, the game object is called Sensor in the ZigFu scenes. All it does is hold the component scripts to talk with OpenNI.

5. Now go to the Project tab and open the OpenNI folder. Make sure the OpenNI Functionality Game Object is selected in the Hierarchy and open in the Inspector. Now click and drag Open NIDepthmap Viewer into the Inspector. Do the same for OpenNIUser Tracker and Open NIUsers Radar and Open NISingle Skeleton Controller.

6. We now need to connect our OpenNI Tracker to our Open NIUsers Radar to make our Radar work. Simply select and drag the Open NIUser Tracker onto the Open NIUsers Radar script. Figure 7-7 shows the correct configuration.

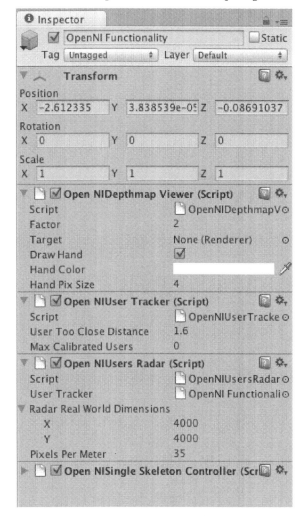

Figure 7-7. *OpenNI User Tracker configuration*

Now that you've tied in the necessary OpenNI functionality, you can move on to make a basic skeleton.

Task 2. Making the Basic Skeleton

Let's get started creating our first skeleton. Here are the steps to follow:

1.   Create an empty game object from the Main menu. Select the following option to do that: Main Menu ➤ Game Object ➤ Create Empty.

2.   Your new empty game object will now be in the Hierarchy tab. Select the object and Ctr+right-click. Choose Rename. Rename the object Custom Skeleton.

3.   Now create a new object, a sphere, as follows: Main Menu ➤ Game Object ➤ Create Other ➤ Sphere.

4.   Now add the sphere to the Custom Skeleton in the Hierarchy. Simply select the sphere and drag it on the words Custom Skeleton. A black arrow will appear while you drag. When you see the back arrow, drop the object.

5.   The Custom Skeleton should have a drop-down arrow next to it, and the sphere should be located within it. This sphere will be our head. Let's rename it Head to match. Rename by pressing Ctr+right-click and then select the Rename option.

6.   Select the sphere and move it upward using the Move tool. The Move tool is automatically activated when an object is selected. Click the green arrow and move the sphere upward in Y space.

7.   Repeat steps 3-6 for each of the two hands. Create two new spheres, add them to the Custom Skeleton, and rename them. Then position them. Since the location of these objects is going to actually be generated by the user, these positions are only for the game developers' benefit when not in Play mode.

▓ **Note** This process of creating objects that are part of a larger object is called parenting. We are adding the sphere objects as children of the Custom Skeleton, their parent.

---

8.   Create two cubes for the left and right shoulders. Do exactly the same as you did for the spheres, but choose to create cubes instead: Main Menu ➤ Game Object ➤ Create Other ➤ Cube.

The Hierarchy tab now should look like the one shown in Figure 7-8.

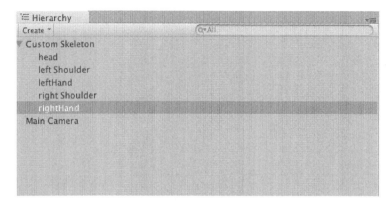

Figure 7-8. *Custom skeleton hierarchy after adding the three spheres and two cubes*

End this task by lighting the scene. Do that by adding a directional light from the following menu option: Main Menu ➤ Create Other ➤ Directional Light.

Task 3. Connecting the Pieces Together

Now it's time to make the skeleton work by linking in the game objects and components. Here's what to do:

1. First, you'll connect the Custom Skeleton Game Object to the OpenNI Skeleton. (ZigFu makes this process nearly effortless.) Go to the Project tab, open the OpenNI folder, and then open the Scripts subfolder. Scroll until Open NISkeleton is visible. Select it and drag it onto the Custom Skeleton Game Object just as we did for the spheres and cube.

2. Next you must connect the objects (the shapes we created earlier) in the Custom Skeleton to the appropriate joints in Open NISkeleton. Select Custom Skeleton in the Hierarchy tab. In the Inspector tab, there should be the script for Open NISkeleton. Click the arrow next to this script to expose all the joints. Select and drag the Head created in Unity in Custom Skeleton in the Hierarchy tab onto the Head in the Open NISkeleton script. Your result should look like Figure 7-9. Especially note the second item, the Head item, in the list in the bottom section of the figure.

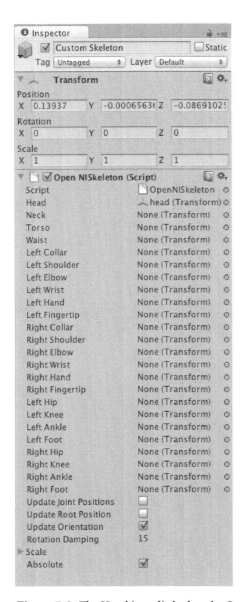

Figure 7-9. The Head item linked to the Open NISkeleton script

3. Repeat Step 2 for the Right Hand, Left Hand, Right Shoulder, and Left Shoulder. If the Inspector changes to the selected object in the Hierarchy tab such as the Cube or Sphere, simply click and drag a little bit faster.

4.   After the list of joints, there are three check boxes that tell Unity how to move these objects' Transform in relation to the skeleton. Set these check boxes as follows:

Update Joint Positions: Check this box. This box allows the object's Transform to change to match the rotation of the joints on the skeleton. If a model was created in a 3D package, there is no need to check this because most likely there will no need to move joint position, just rotate the joints.

Update Root Position: This will update the game object (Custom Skeleton) in relation to the user in 3D space. If this is checked, the objects will move in 3D space with the user; otherwise, the game object will stay in a fixed position, even though the joints will move.

Update Orientation: Check this box. This updates the rotation of the joints in 3D space.

5.   The remaining option is for Scale. Expand this menu. The default unit of measurement in OpenNI is millimeters and in Unity is in meters. This option scales the game object approximately. For this exercise, change the scale of X, Y, and Z to 0.008.

6.   Now select OpenNI Functionality in your Hierarchy tab so that you can access its components in the Inspector. In the Inspector, find the OpenNISingle Skeleton Controller script. Open the arrow to expose all of this component's properties. Drag the Custom Skeleton from the Hierarchy tab onto the Skeletons property of the OpenNISingle Skeleton Controller.

7.   Lastly, drag the OpenNI Functionality onto the OpenNISingle Skeleton Controller User Tracker.

That was the magic sauce! Now run the scene and perform the calibration pose. After the tracker latches onto your skeleton, you should see results like those in Figure 7-10.

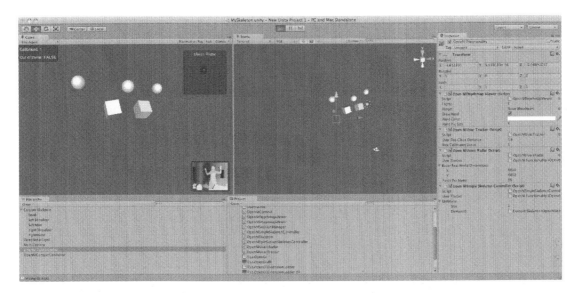

Figure 7-10. *The custom skeleton in operation*

Creating a Custom Hand Tracker

For the last order of business, let's make a custom hand-tracker example from scratch. Create a new scene and call it MyScene. Now add a cube game object to the scene and open it in the Hierarchy tab. Open the HandpointControl folder. Select the Follow Hand Point script onto the Cube in the Inspector. Play the scene, do the calibration, and voilà—hand tracking. ZigFu can be that simple. Figure 7-11 shows the hand-tracking scene in operation.

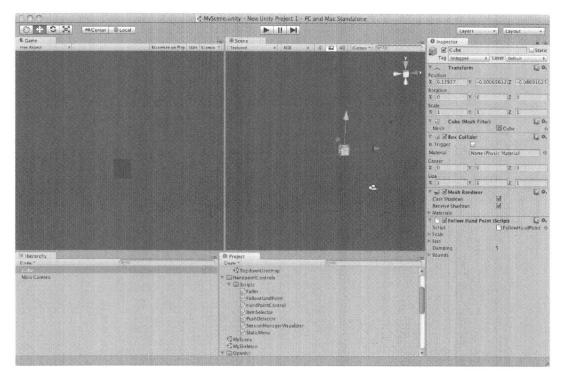

Figure 7-11. *The hand-tracker scene*

On a final note, ZigFu are developers worth watching. Other interesting projects they have include a set of Unity scripts for the official Microsoft SDK that are calibration free as of today.

`http://groups.google.com/group/unitykinect/browse_thread/thread/7217ea5eaf4d37e2`

In addition, the next thing they plan on doing is wrapping the Beckon SDK with OpenNI, and then Unity will work seamlessly with any sensor supported by Beckon. Expanded controller free games and interfaces are becoming more and more common, and even by the day this book is released, new updates will be available. In summary, developing games and experiences that go beyond mice and controllers positions any creator at the front of user experience design.

CHAPTER 8

Microsoft's Kinect SDK

Microsoft Research launched its Kinect for Windows Software Development Kit (SDK) with great fanfare on June 16, 2011, a little more than seven months after the device was released into the wild. While Microsoft perhaps never intended to support development for the Kinect on Windows and was likely surprised by the intensive interest the device generated, the company is aggressively supporting the platform now—you'll want to watch for updates from Microsoft Research as no print book can possibly keep abreast of the latest developments:

`http://research.microsoft.com/kinectsdk/`

That said, there's enough to the Kinect SDK and associated resources (such as the Coding4Fun Kinect Toolkit, which includes helper and example code) to get you up and running building apps with some of the most sophisticated and mature Kinect code available. The resources covered here offer a great way for C#, C++, and Visual Basic developers—as well as intrepid beginners—to start using the Kinect with Microsoft's wonderfully robust code for user segmentation, skeletal tracking, and even speech recognition. (The Windows SDK is the best toolset available if you want to tap into the Kinect's multimicrophone array, for example.)

Note Coding for Windows is not the same as coding for Xbox. Microsoft has a separate programming framework called XNA and development environment called Game Studio for developers to create indie games for Xbox Live. As of this writing, Kinect functionalities have **not** been exposed in XNA, though company insiders say that's forthcoming. The Kinect SDK covered in this chapter empowers you to created Kinect apps for only the Windows platform, not Xbox.

Coding4Fun

Often the best way to learn a new tool is to look at examples of how other folks use it to implement their apps, thought experiments, and other feats of code. To that end, there's Coding4Fun (Figure 8-1), a Microsoft site dedicated to enthusiast adventures with the company's technologies. To mark the launch of the Kinect SDK in June 2011, Microsoft held a camp at the Microsoft campus in Redmond, Washington, where 30-odd developers were given a Kinect, the SDK, and 24 hours to create sweet little apps that demonstrate the possibilities of this new toolset. The apps became the basis of Microsoft's showcase/repository of Kinect projects on Coding4Fun, which is well worth checking out before, during, or after you read this chapter:

`http://channel9.msdn.com/coding4fun/kinect`

New projects and examples are frequently posted on the Coding4Fun site, often with source code, so it's the first place to look in case there's a project out there that can jump-start your own Kinect-for-Windows project.

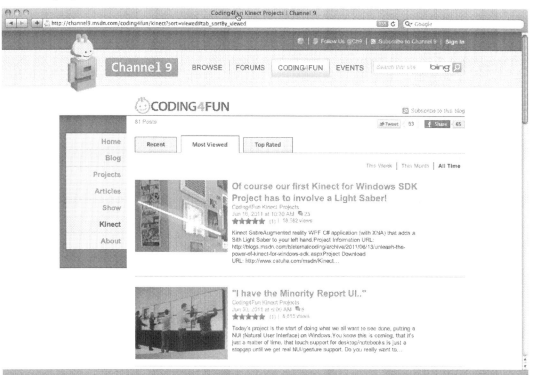

Figure 8-1. The Coding4Fun Kinect section

Kinect SDK Pros and Cons

The upside to using Microsoft's SDK is considerable. It gives you better Application Programming Interfaces (APIs) than any other package for accessing Kinect's specific hardware capabilities, such as its four-element microphone array. The SDK also ships with Microsoft's Kinect runtime and other supporting software, which give you the power of Microsoft's engineering and algorithms for implementing user segmentation, skeletal tracking, and (if you include the Speech SDK) voice control, all without leaving Windows's powerful application frameworks.

These components you get from the Kinect SDK are, in a word, bad ass. We've run the various middleware discussed elsewhere in the book such as PrimeSense's open source OpenNI, and used them to implement some of the same functionality. While all of this software is amazing, our experience put Microsoft's Kinect code at the top performance-wise for its low-latency responsiveness and the pure magic of its calibration-free skeletal tracking algorithm.

The downside—at least, for some of you—is that all you can really do with Microsoft's SDK right now is "code for fun" because the license permits only limited, noncommercial use of the software. (As you probably can guess, the company says that a commercial-use license is forthcoming, though the price and terms are anyone's guess.) Moreover, if you're new to programming C#, C++, or Visual Basic or to using an integrated development environment (IDE), the excellent-but-formidable Microsoft Visual Studio and supported languages may well scare off the fainthearted.

For the rest of you, put some coffee on.

Getting Started with the Kinect SDK

To set up a Kinect development environment on Windows, you're going to need a Kinect, an open USB port, and Windows 7, plus a lot of (no-cost) software from Microsoft, including the appropriate Visual Studio edition for your programming language of choice and the Kinect SDK itself from Microsoft Research. Everything you need is itemized below under "Requirements," along with some common gotchas.

Requirements

The requirements for working with the Kinect SDK are many but manageable. And the only costs should be your PC and the Kinect. Note that I use the term "PC" inclusively—I was able to run everything in this chapter on a Mac Mini running Windows 7 on Bootcamp. However, as of this writing, you cannot use the Kinect SDK via a virtual machine like Parallels or VMware. Word to the wise.

System

You'll need a fairly current PC to run the software described in this chapter: a dual-core, 2.66 GHz or faster processor; Windows 7–compatible graphics card that supports DirectX 9.0c capabilities (which were released in August 2004, so if your computer is less than five years old running Windows 7, you're probably good); and at least 2 GB of RAM (4 GB is recommended). And of course, you need a Kinect sensor! But hopefully you squared that away in Chapter 1.

Software-wise, you must be running Windows 7, either the 64- or 32-bit version, and you're going to need to know which version you have so that you can download the correct version of the SDK. To find out which version you have, check out Control Panel ➤ System and Security ➤ System and scan down to

153

where it says "System type." You should see either "64-bit Operating System" or "32-bit Operating System."

Visual Studio 2010

If you're a Windows developer, you probably have a version of Visual Studio already installed. Any 2010 edition will suffice, and the Express editions are recommended here simply because they're free. To download yours, just browse to:

```
http://www.microsoft.com/visualstudio
```

Under the Products tab, click Visual Basic Express, Visual C# Express, or Visual C++ Express depending on which language you plan to code in. Since many of the examples available online are written in C#, we'll use Visual C# Express here. That way, we'll be all set up to pull down and pull apart most of the code we find on the interwebs. Click Install Now to download and install Visual C# Express. Just go with the default installation options unless you have some personal reason for changing them.

Additional Frameworks and Supporting Software

.NET Framework

Without a doubt, you need the .NET 4.0 framework for building your apps in Visual Studio. The framework is typically bundled with Visual Studio, but if not, download and run the installer—it's fairly large and can take some time:

```
http://msdn.microsoft.com/en-us/netframework/aa569263
```

Beyond that, the other supporting software described here is optional. Still, if you plan on exploring Kinect for Windows in depth, you might as well get this software installed now, as it is used in some of the examples included with the SDK, as well as many third-party examples found online.

DirectX Runtime and SDK

Microsoft's DirectX software consists of a number of libraries largely used to handle media and graphics functions necessary for creating games. The Sample Shape Game that ships with the Kinect SDK (below), for example, uses DirectX.
 Microsoft DirectX SDK (June 2010 or later version):

```
http://www.microsoft.com/download/en/details.aspx?id=6812
```

And the current DirectX end-user runtime:

```
http://www.microsoft.com/download/en/details.aspx?id=35
```

Microsoft's Speech Platform

Again, these components are optional. However, they do differentiate Microsoft's offering for Kinect developers from the other packages described in this book. If you plan on integrating speech recognition in your app or just want to play around with this feature of the Sample Shape Game, download these packages and run the installers. Note that even if you are on a 64-bit machine, you must download the x86 (32-bit) edition of the Speech Platform software. The 64-bit version will not work:

Microsoft Speech Platform SDK, version 10.2 (x86 edition)
http://www.microsoft.com/download/en/details.aspx?id=14373

Microsoft Speech Platform Runtime, version 10.2 (x86 edition)
http://www.microsoft.com/download/en/details.aspx?id=10208

Microsoft Kinect Speech Platform (US English version)
http://go.microsoft.com/fwlink/?LinkId=220942

The Kinect SDK and Coding4Fun Kinect Toolkit

Finally, the Kinect stuff! Browse to the Kinect SDK landing page (below) and click Download. Here you need to choose the 32- or 64-bit version depending on your operating system as described under "System" above. The URL for the Kinect SDK landing page is:

http://research.microsoft.com/kinectsdk/

Run the installer. When it is finished, you're ready to launch Visual Studio (in our case, Visual C# Express) and start using the Kinect SDK.

However, there's one final optional piece of software that you probably want to download. The Coding4Fun Kinect Toolkit wraps some typical tasks we do with Kinect data into simpler function calls—such as converting raw data into a bitmapped image—making the code you have to write simpler and cleaner. This library is used in some of the samples included with the SDK and is a recommended addition to your setup. You can download the library here:

http://c4fkinect.codeplex.com/

Choose the zipped current release, download it, and extract it. There's no installer program for the Coding4Fun library. Instead, we have to add a reference to it in each project in which we want to use the library. This is a task to do inside Visual Studio, our development environment, when setting up a new Kinect project, as detailed below. For now, just stash the downloaded, unarchived library wherever you want to keep it, such as inside the Visual Studio 2010 folder that should now appear in your Documents folder.

Running and Troubleshooting the Samples

Before we try to build our own code, we should try running the two compiled samples included with the SDK to make sure everything's working as expected. You should see that the SDK is installed by looking for it under Programs in the Start menu. There are two compiled sample applications now under Programs ➤ Kinect for Windows SDK ➤ Sample Skeletal Viewer and Programs ➤ Kinect for Windows SDK ➤ Sample Shape Game in the Start menu. Let's launch the Sample Skeletal Viewer. You should see results similar to those in Figure 8-2.

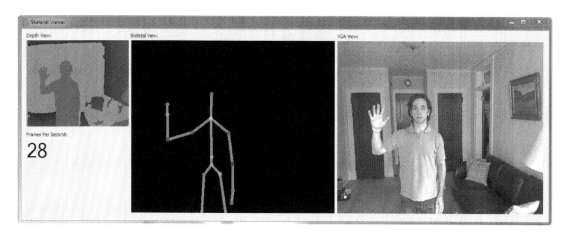

Figure 8-2. The working Sample Skeletal Viewer program included with the Kinect SDK

If you get an alert like "NuiInitalize Failed" or see the window in Figure 8-3, something is amiss:

Figure 8-3. The Sample Skeletal Viewer program failing

In that case, it's time to troubleshoot. As always, make sure the Kinect is plugged into your PC and the power cord is connected to a wall socket. If you have many USB devices or use a USB hub, you're going to have to make room for the Kinect: Either plug it directly into one of the ports on the PC itself, or if it must be on a hub, make sure the Kinect not sharing the hub with any other high-throughput USB devices.

Another potential source of trouble is the drivers. If you installed third-party device drivers for the Kinect to run any of the other packages or examples in this book, the new ones included with the Kinect SDK should supersede the third-party drivers. However, if there is a conflict, you may need to uninstall the other drivers in the Device Manager (see below).

When the Kinect is connected the first time after the SDK has been installed, Windows automagically installs drivers for the various hardware components, which are now identified as the Microsoft Kinect Device, Microsoft Kinect Camera, and Microsoft Kinect Audio Array Control. If you take a look at the Device Manager, you should find these three components under a Microsoft Kinect list item. If, however, you still see Xbox NUI Motor, XBox NUI Camera, and XBox NUI Audio under the generic Human Interface Components list item, you will want to right-click each one and select Uninstall.

Finally, you may also need to uninstall and reinstall the Kinect SDK and drivers after making these changes. Once you see Microsoft Kinect and its three components here in the Device Manager, you should be golden. But if you're still not, you will need to check out the forums online to troubleshoot your particular issue.

Setting Up New Kinect Projects

If you're new to Windows development, you may want to bookmark this section as you'll have to perform the steps we cover here every time you set up a new project in Visual C# Express in which you want to use the Kinect SDK.

Basically, the process is this:

1. Create a new Windows Presentation Foundation (WPF) project.

2. Add references to the Kinect SDK and the Coding4Fun Kinect library.

3. Add "using" statements to tell our code what libraries we're using.

4. Create standard Loaded and Closed events in our application to initialize and uninitialize the resources that Visual Studio uses when running a Kinect application.

Similar steps are also covered in a Quickstart video series on the Microsoft Research site.

Step 1: Create a New Project

To create a new WPF project in Visual C# Express, just launch the application and choose File ➤ New Project... or New Project... from the home screen. In the dialog window that opens, choose WPF Application, as shown in Figure 8-4.

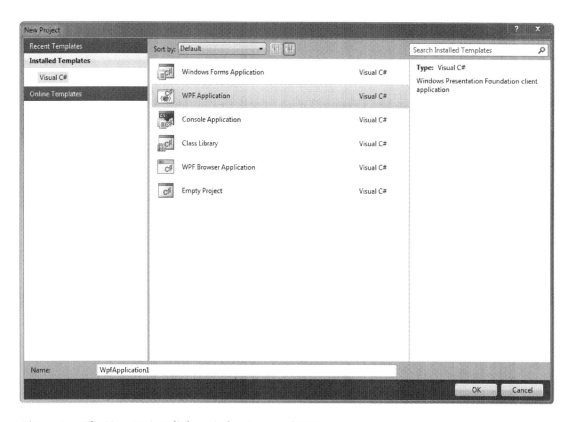

Figure 8-4. *The New Project dialog window in Visual C# Express*

Windows Presentation Foundation is simply the system Windows uses to organize and link user interface elements in Windows applications. XML (or XAML) files are at the heart of WPF—you'll see one called MainWindow.Xaml when your new project is created.

Step 2: Add References to the Kinect SDK and Coding4Fun

Next, we want to add references to the code we're going to use in the project. If this is your first time using a Visual Studio program, it's worth exploring the layout of your new project window and identifying what's what. Figure 8-5 shows the window.

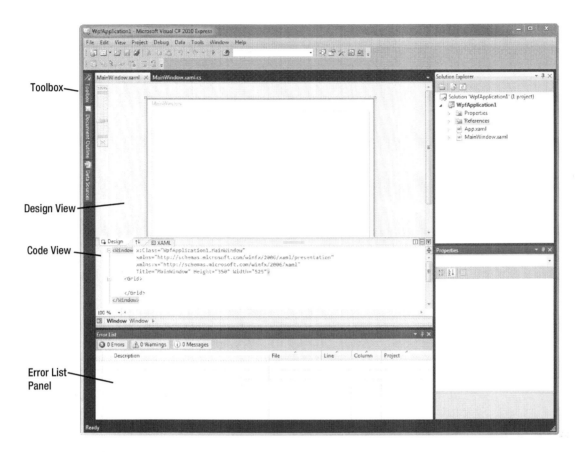

Toolbox

Design View

Code View

Error List
Panel

Figure 8-5. *The New Project window*

To add a reference, which is just an external resource to be used by your application or "Solution," note the list item References in the Solution Explorer panel at the upper right of the window. Right-click References and choose Add Reference… In the dialog box that opens, shown in Figure 8-6, scan down under the .NET tab for the component named Microsoft.Research.Kinect, select it, and click OK.

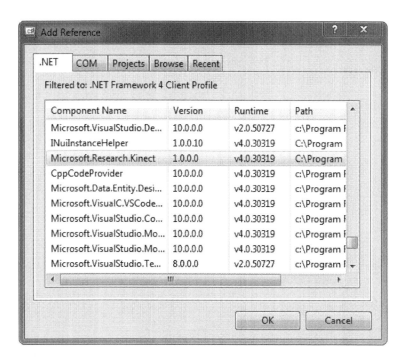

Figure 8-6. *The Add Reference dialog for adding the SDK to a project*

Excellent: one down, one to go! Now take the same steps to add the Coding4Fun Kinect Toolkit. Only this time, in the Add Reference dialog box (again, Figure 8-6), choose the Browse tab and browse to the location on your computer where you stashed the extracted Coding4Fun files. In the Coding4Fun.Kinect folder, select Coding4Fun.Kinect.Wpf.dll and click OK. Bingo! Your References list in the Solution Explorer should now look like Figure 8-7:

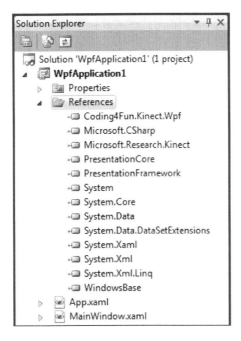

Figure 8-7. *The list of references in the project window's Solution Explorer panel after the SDK and Coding4Fun have been added*

Step 3: Add "Using" Statements

At long last, we're ready to code! You're going to want to switch from editing the XAML file to editing the C# ("C-Sharp") file called MainWindow.xaml.cs. Do this by clicking the tab MainWindow.xaml.cs in the main area of the project. You should see the code shown in Figure 8-8.

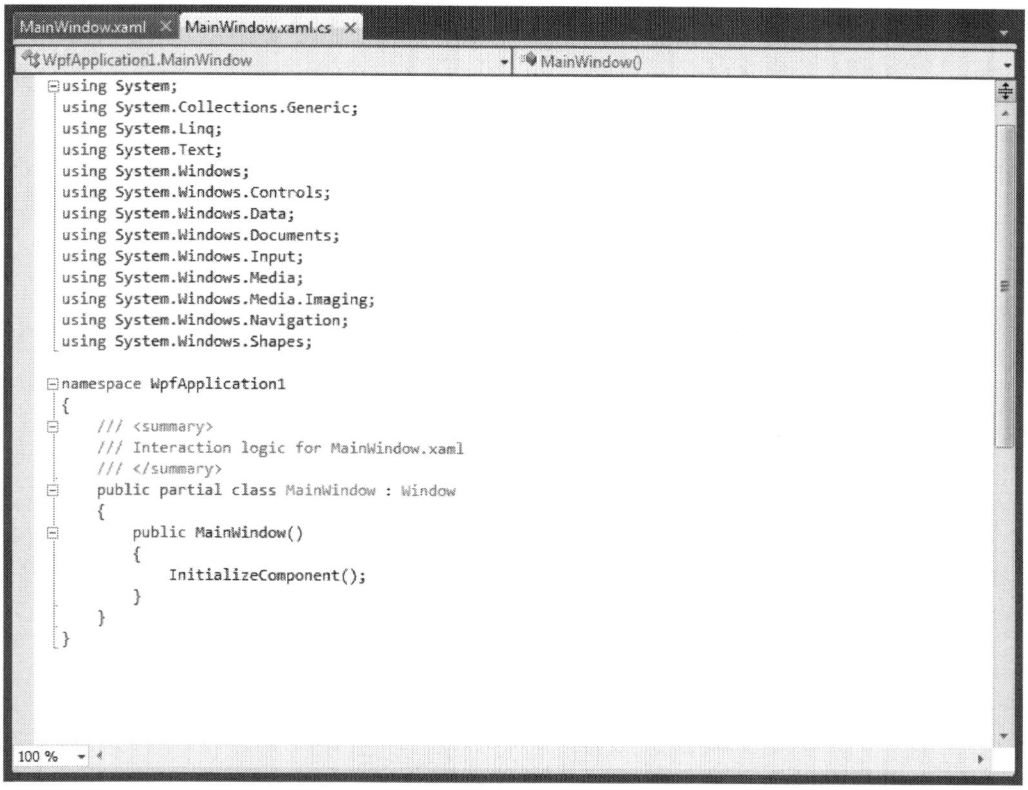

Figure 8-8. The C# code in MainWindow.xaml.cs

You'll see "using" statements already in place. Place your cursor after the last one, make a new line, and type:

```
using Microsoft.Research.Kinect.Nui;
using Microsoft.Research.Kinect.Audio;
using Coding4Fun.Kinect.Wpf;
```

Done and done. (Don't type that, though!)

Step 4. Create Loaded and Closed Events

One more step for our Kinect project template to be complete! The reason for this step is simple: we need to make sure we initialize and uninitialize the Kinect runtime in every application that uses it, lest chaos (or at least, poor memory management) ensues. So, we're going to add functions that will initialize it for us whenever our application window is loaded and uninitialize it whenever the window is closed.

To do so, switch back to the XAML file tab and look at the Properties panel at the bottom right of the project window. Click the Events tab and scan down the alphabetical list of events until you see the Loaded event shown in Figure 8-9.

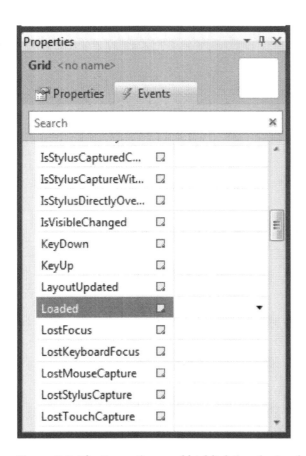

Figure 8-9. The Properties panel highlighting the Loaded event

Double-click the Loaded event. Visual Studio automatically creates an empty event callback function and switches back to your .cs file where the function lives:

```
private void Window_Loaded(object sender, RoutedEventArgs e)
    {

    }
```

Now, repeat these steps to add a Closed event to your application, which adds the `Window_Closed` event callback function to your .cs file. All we need to do is put up our initialization and uninitialization code, and we're done. Fortunately, the Kinect SDK makes this code super simple.

Put your cursor before (and outside) the `Window_Loaded` function and give your Kinect runtime a name like this:

```
Runtime kinect = new Runtime();
```

Now inside the `Window_Loaded` function, initialize the runtime with the `intialize()` function, which takes configuration options as arguments separated by the "|" character. We're simply telling the application to use the Kinect's RGB color camera and raw depth:

```
kinect.Initialize(RuntimeOptions.UseColor | RuntimeOptions.UseDepth);
```

Finally, add an `uninitalize()` function call inside the `Window_Closed` function:

```
kinect.Uninitialize();
```

When you're done, the code in your .cs file should look about like this:

```
using System;
using System.Collections.Generic;
using System.Linq;
using System.Text;
using System.Windows;
using System.Windows.Controls;
using System.Windows.Data;
using System.Windows.Documents;
using System.Windows.Input;
using System.Windows.Media;
using System.Windows.Media.Imaging;
using System.Windows.Navigation;
using System.Windows.Shapes;
using Microsoft.Research.Kinect.Nui;
using Microsoft.Research.Kinect.Audio;
using Coding4Fun.Kinect.Wpf;

namespace WpfApplication1
{
    /// <summary>
    /// Interaction logic for MainWindow.xaml
    /// </summary>
    public partial class MainWindow : Window
    {
        public MainWindow()
        {
            InitializeComponent();
        }

        Runtime kinect = new Runtime();
        private void Window_Loaded(object sender, RoutedEventArgs e)
        {
            kinect.Initialize(RuntimeOptions.UseColor | RuntimeOptions.UseDepth);
        }

        private void Window_Closed(object sender, EventArgs e)
        {
            kinect.Uninitialize();
        }

    }
}
```

Sweet! You can successfully build and run/debug this application now, which you should do to make sure there are no syntax mistakes. Click the green arrow shown in Figure 8-10.

Build and Debug

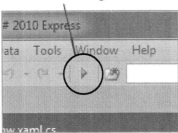

Figure 8-10. *The green arrow to initiate a build and debug sequence*

Of course, the application does absolutely *nothing*! Nothing you can *see*, anyway. But it is safely initializing and uninitializing the Kinect runtime so that now any code we want to sandwich between the Loaded and the Closed events will execute properly. This is the basic template setup we'll want to use for each new Kinect project we work on, so you might just save it somewhere to be copied as needed.

Now, we build.

Building a Simple Application

Building a Kinect application is now just a matter of laying out our user interface in the XAML file (which we can do easily with the authoring tools in Visual Studio) and putting some code to execute between the Loaded and Closed events we just addressed (which the Coding4Fun Toolkit is going to make a snap). Let's do it.

Deciding What to Build

Like many of the bootstrap examples we've covered, let's say we just want to built a simple app along the lines of the Sample Skeletal Viewer, but we want to do it from scratch so that we really learn what it takes. (The source for the samples is provided with the SDK, but they don't utilize the Coding4Fun helper library and are therefore a bit more complex.) Essentially, we want to create an app that gets the major raw data streams (color and depth images), does some of the analysis we need to make that data more useful (user segmentation and skeletal tracking), and renders it to the screen. How do we do it?

Laying Out the UI

Starting from the template we created in the last section, select the MainWindow.XAML tab. Note in the design view (upper) panel that there's a white Main Window box. This represents the main application window that will sit right inside the chrome when you launch your app.

If you click the Main Window box, handles appear at the corners that you can click and drag to resize it as in Figure 8-11. Let's just do a little clicking and dragging to lay out the main window for our application and any objects in it just the way we want.

Figure 8-11. *The design view of the XAML file lets you move and resize objects with the mouse*

I dragged the corners of my main window out to a width of 800 pixels and a height of 350 pixels. You can see the attribute values in the code view change when you release the mouse, and you can modify them in code as well as in the Properties panel at the bottom left of the project window. In code view, for example, the attributes of my Window tag look like this:

```
Title="MainWindow" Height="350" Width="800" Closed="Window_Closed" Loaded="Window_Loaded"
```

Now open up the Toolbox as in Figure 8-12 in the upper left of the project window (it is identified in the overview of the project window earlier in this chapter) and drag an image object from the palette of "tools" onto the main window. As we did with the main window, size the image object using the handles, the Properties panel, or the XAML code. Just make sure to accommodate the aspect ratio of the 640 × 480 resolution Kinect. For example, I sized mine to 320 pixels by 240 pixels.

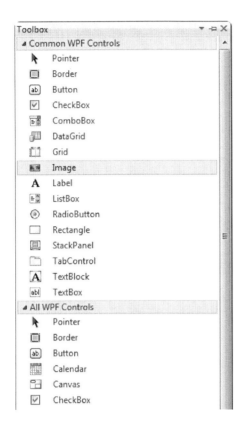

Figure 8-12. *The Toolbox in Visual Studio, with an image object highlighted*

You can then copy and paste another instance of the image object onto the main window so that we have one for the RGB image and one for the depth image. Arrange them however you like, and notice that the Properties panel for the selected object gives its default name (e.g., "image1," "image2," etc.). You can change these names if you want, but these are the names we'll be using to target these objects programmatically in code. Speaking of which, let's leave our layout as is and start to wire it up in the .cs file.

Wiring Up the UI with Code

Here's how we're going to make this work: We'll use events from the Kinect runtime to trigger a function whenever there's a new frame of image data from the RGB camera and another function whenever there's a new frame of depth data. These functions will update the content of the appropriate image object in the main window, and we'll have an application that collects and renders the major data streams from the Kinect, just like that.

So, below our initialization of the Kinect runtime inside the `Window_Loaded` function, type in some code to listen for the new frame or `FrameReady` events and tie them to appropriate callback functions, which we'll define later:

```
kinect.VideoFrameReady += new EventHandler<ImageFrameReadyEventArgs>(kinect_VideoFrameReady);
kinect.DepthFrameReady += new EventHandler<ImageFrameReadyEventArgs>(kinect_DepthFrameReady);
```

Next, we have to open these data streams from the Kinect device to start generating images. Simply add:

```
kinect.VideoStream.Open(ImageStreamType.Video, 2, ImageResolution.Resolution640x480,
ImageType.Color);
kinect.DepthStream.Open(ImageStreamType.Depth, 2, ImageResolution.Resolution320x240,
ImageType.Depth);
```

This code is fairly self-explanatory: we're using built-in settings and types to configure and start each data stream. The second argument in the Stream.Open() function (i.e., the "2") is the only obscure one: it refers to the PoolSize, or the number of buffers to use for playback of the stream data. It must be a number from 1 to 4. We chose 2: one buffer to display the current frame and one buffer to load the new frame. Adding more buffers introduces latency but can give smoother playback of the data.

Finally, to get this application working, we need to define the functions we tied to the FrameReady events, the kinect_VideoFrameReady and kinect_DepthFrameReady functions. Again, these functions simply need to update our image objects with the image data from the color and depth streams from the Kinect. Using the ToBitmapSource() function available to us from Coding4Fun, this is quite easy:

```
void kinect_VideoFrameReady(object sender, ImageFrameReadyEventArgs e)
{
        image1.Source = e.ImageFrame.ToBitmapSource();
}

void kinect_DepthFrameReady(object sender, ImageFrameReadyEventArgs e)
{
        image2.Source = e.ImageFrame.ToBitmapSource();
}
```

The names "image1" and "image2," you'll recall, are the defaults given to the image objects we dragged into our main window from the Toolbox. If you changed these names in the XAML file, you need to change them here in the code, too. With that done, we're ready to build and run this project. You should get an output window like that in Figure 8-13.

Figure 8-13. *Color and depth images*

That was easy! But it gives us nothing that we can't get with libfreenect. Where's the magic? Good question. Let's see if we can add some of Microsoft's special sauce!

First, we can try getting a depth image that identifies people in the scene in front of the Kinect, a task commonly called *user segmentation* but might be called *player segmentation* in the context of the Microsoft APIs. With the Kinect SDK, we can add player segmentation just by changing our runtime configuration and depth image type from Depth to DepthAndPlayerIndex throughout the code. That means changing the initialization to:

```
kinect.Initialize(RuntimeOptions.UseColor | RuntimeOptions.UseDepthAndPlayerIndex);
```

And changing the image type in the `DepthStream.Open()` like so:

```
kinect.DepthStream.Open(ImageStreamType.Depth, 2, ImageResolution.Resolution320x240,
ImageType.DepthAndPlayerIndex);
```

And we can get something like the image in Figure 8-14, where the "player" is now segmented in the scene and given a color overlay.

Figure 8-14. *Color and DepthAndPlayerIndex images*

Now, what about proper skeletal tracking, the stuff that makes actual gameplay using the Kinect sensor possible? In essence, implementing skeletal tracking in your application is no more difficult than implementing the color and depth image functionalities as above. Just add an option to the runtime configuration and a `SkeletonFrameReady` event and callback. In the `Window_Loaded` function, that's changing/adding two lines:

```
kinect.Initialize(RuntimeOptions.UseColor | RuntimeOptions.UseDepthAndPlayerIndex |
RuntimeOptions.UseSkeletalTracking);
SkeletonFrameReady += new
EventHandler<SkeletonFrameReadyEventArgs>(kinect_SkeletonFrameReady);
```

In practice, of course, to use the skeleton information, you need to write a `kinect_SkeletonFrameReady` function that uses the data intelligently, mapping the body joints to objects and controllers in the application, etc. Following is a simplified version of the full Skeletal Viewer code that maps and draws that data to the screen, producing a result similar to that in Figure 8-15 (after adding a third image object to display the skeleton):

Figure 8-15. *Displaying the skeleton in the center of the window*

The code, partially borrowed from the Sample Skeletal Viewer, looks something like this:

```
using System;
using System.Collections.Generic;
using System.Linq;
using System.Text;
using System.Windows;
using System.Windows.Controls;
using System.Windows.Data;
using System.Windows.Documents;
using System.Windows.Input;
using System.Windows.Media;
using System.Windows.Media.Imaging;
using System.Windows.Navigation;
using System.Windows.Shapes;
using Microsoft.Research.Kinect.Nui;
using Microsoft.Research.Kinect.Audio;
using Coding4Fun.Kinect.Wpf;

namespace WpfApplication1
{
    /// <summary>
    /// Interaction logic for MainWindow.xaml
    /// </summary>
    public partial class MainWindow : Window
    {
        public MainWindow()
        {
```

```
        InitializeComponent();
    }

    Runtime kinect = new Runtime();

    private void Window_Loaded(object sender, RoutedEventArgs e)
    {
        kinect.Initialize(RuntimeOptions.UseColor | RuntimeOptions.UseDepthAndPlayerIndex
| RuntimeOptions.UseSkeletalTracking);
        kinect.VideoFrameReady += new
EventHandler<ImageFrameReadyEventArgs>(kinect_VideoFrameReady);
        kinect.DepthFrameReady += new
EventHandler<ImageFrameReadyEventArgs>(kinect_DepthFrameReady);
        kinect.SkeletonFrameReady += new
EventHandler<SkeletonFrameReadyEventArgs>(kinect_SkeletonFrameReady);
        kinect.VideoStream.Open(ImageStreamType.Video, 2,
ImageResolution.Resolution640x480, ImageType.Color);
        kinect.DepthStream.Open(ImageStreamType.Depth, 2,
ImageResolution.Resolution320x240, ImageType.DepthAndPlayerIndex);
    }

    void kinect_VideoFrameReady(object sender, ImageFrameReadyEventArgs e)
    {
        image1.Source = e.ImageFrame.ToBitmapSource();
    }

    void kinect_DepthFrameReady(object sender, ImageFrameReadyEventArgs e)
    {
        image2.Source = e.ImageFrame.ToBitmapSource();
    }

    void kinect_SkeletonFrameReady(object sender, SkeletonFrameReadyEventArgs e)
    {
        SkeletonFrame skeletonFrame = e.SkeletonFrame;
        int iSkeleton = 0;
        Brush[] brushes = new Brush[6];
        brushes[0] = new SolidColorBrush(Color.FromRgb(255, 0, 0));
        brushes[1] = new SolidColorBrush(Color.FromRgb(0, 255, 0));
        brushes[2] = new SolidColorBrush(Color.FromRgb(64, 255, 255));
        brushes[3] = new SolidColorBrush(Color.FromRgb(255, 255, 64));
        brushes[4] = new SolidColorBrush(Color.FromRgb(255, 64, 255));
        brushes[5] = new SolidColorBrush(Color.FromRgb(128, 128, 255));

        canvas1.Children.Clear();
        foreach (SkeletonData data in skeletonFrame.Skeletons)
        {
            if (SkeletonTrackingState.Tracked == data.TrackingState)
            {
                // Draw bones
                Brush brush = brushes[iSkeleton % brushes.Length];
                canvas1.Children.Add(getBodySegment(data.Joints, brush, JointID.HipCenter,
JointID.Spine, JointID.ShoulderCenter, JointID.Head));
```

```
                        canvas1.Children.Add(getBodySegment(data.Joints, brush,
JointID.ShoulderCenter, JointID.ShoulderLeft, JointID.ElbowLeft, JointID.WristLeft,
JointID.HandLeft));
                        canvas1.Children.Add(getBodySegment(data.Joints, brush,
JointID.ShoulderCenter, JointID.ShoulderRight, JointID.ElbowRight, JointID.WristRight,
JointID.HandRight));
                        canvas1.Children.Add(getBodySegment(data.Joints, brush, JointID.HipCenter,
JointID.HipLeft, JointID.KneeLeft, JointID.AnkleLeft, JointID.FootLeft));
                        canvas1.Children.Add(getBodySegment(data.Joints, brush, JointID.HipCenter,
JointID.HipRight, JointID.KneeRight, JointID.AnkleRight, JointID.FootRight));

                    // Draw joints
                    foreach (Joint joint in data.Joints)
                    {
                        Point jointPos = getDisplayPosition(joint);
                        Line jointLine = new Line();
                        jointLine.X1 = jointPos.X - 3;
                        jointLine.X2 = jointLine.X1 + 6;
                        jointLine.Y1 = jointLine.Y2 = jointPos.Y;
                        jointLine.Stroke = brushes[0];
                        jointLine.StrokeThickness = 6;
                        canvas1.Children.Add(jointLine);
                    }
                }
                iSkeleton++;
            } // for each skeleton
        }

        private Point getDisplayPosition(Joint joint)
        {
            float depthX, depthY;
            kinect.SkeletonEngine.SkeletonToDepthImage(joint.Position, out depthX, out
depthY);
            depthX = depthX * 320; //convert to 320, 240 space
            depthY = depthY * 240; //convert to 320, 240 space
            int colorX, colorY;
            ImageViewArea iv = new ImageViewArea();
            // only ImageResolution.Resolution640x480 is supported at this point

kinect.NuiCamera.GetColorPixelCoordinatesFromDepthPixel(ImageResolution.Resolution640x480, iv,
(int)depthX, (int)depthY, (short)0, out colorX, out colorY);

            // map back to skeleton.Width & skeleton.Height
            return new Point((int)(canvas1.Width * colorX / 640.0), (int)(canvas1.Height *
colorY / 480));
        }

        Polyline getBodySegment(Microsoft.Research.Kinect.Nui.JointsCollection joints, Brush
brush, params JointID[] ids)
        {
            PointCollection points = new PointCollection(ids.Length);
            for (int i = 0; i < ids.Length; ++i)
```

```
        {
            points.Add(getDisplayPosition(joints[ids[i]]));
        }

        Polyline polyline = new Polyline();
        polyline.Points = points;
        polyline.Stroke = brush;
        polyline.StrokeThickness = 5;
        return polyline;
    }

    private void Window_Closed(object sender, EventArgs e)
    {
        kinect.Uninitialize();
    }

    }
}
```

Need More?

In this chapter, we've tried to give a detailed introduction to all of the tools needed to build an application with Microsoft's Kinect SDK, but obviously the application presented is rather basic: we used only the Kinect's camera and depth capabilities (not even touching sound) and straight-out-of-the-box user segmentation skeletal tracking.

There's lots more to do, and if the Microsoft toolset appeals to you, no doubt you'll want to do lots more! That's beyond the scope of this book, but there's a growing body of example code out there on the Coding4Fun site and the open Web for you to draw on, much of it tackling specific tasks and use cases. Search around, subscribe to forums, and watch Microsoft, because after a slow start supporting Kinect developers, now they're really going for it!

▨ **Note** For an even deeper treatment of the Microsoft SDK for the Kinect, you can do no better than to grab a copy of Jarrett Webb's and James Ashley's book *Beginning Kinect Programming*. It's also published by Apress.

CHAPTER 9

Volumetric Display Techniques

In this chapter, you will become familiar with the various techniques for the volumetric display of visual imagery. Unlike a traditional 2D screen, or even the newest glasses-based stereoscopic 3D TVs and movie theatre experiences, volumetric technologies providethe viewer with a feeling of "holographic" imagery with varying degrees of motion parallax based on the technique used to recreate a display in natural 3D space. Motion parallax describes the ability to perceive depth based on the movement of the observer relative to multiple stationary objects against a background. Believe it or not, many people cannot actually perceive the 3D effect from stereo glasses because their brains lack full stereovision development. How come these people aren't bumping into things? It's because every slight movement of your head reveals the depth of your surroundings. This feature, not yet available in any mass market 3D solution, is what sets this novel approach apart from glasses-based experiences.

Perhaps the most well-known practical example of a volumetric display from the realm of science fiction is from the original Star Wars movie, when R2D2 displays a recording of Princess Leia telling Obi WanKinobe he's her only hope. Depth-sensing photographic technology, such as the Kinect, effectively captures "holographic"or volumetric video recordings, but doesn't provide a way to display them back into volumetric 3D space. Volumetric displays are the key to projecting these "holographic" experiences back into the dimensionality of everyday life. For the most part still on the edge of research and prohibitively priced for consumers to experience at home, these displays won't make it into your livingroom this year—but the pace of technology's progress takes unexpected leaps, as the Kinect has shown us.

This chapter will cover the full spectrum of novel display types, including those that strictly qualify as volumetric displays and many that do not. It will cover those that contain key aspects, such as motion parallax and multiple views on a screen, and some that have none of those qualities yet receive recognition, as the public erroneously refers to them as "holographic" because their imagery hangs in the air. This is an introduction to display technology that many are unfamiliar with, as little up-to-date information on the topic has been collected on the internet. These innovative approaches will likely be seen more in the future, perhaps in combination, to satisfy the demands of a public having been primed by the Kinect's volumetric camera and who will come to expect more than just a 2D screen for truly immersive experiences.

Static Volume Displays

If you've been through any major American mall or tourist area in the past couple of years, you've likely seen the novelty service that takes a 3D portrait photo, which then gets etched into a clear plastic prism (Figure 9-1), a process known as sub-surface laser engraving. While this isn't a volumetric display that can be updated, it provides a reference point for understanding the first class of displays known as *static volume* displays.

Figure 9-1. *A Sub-Surface Laser Engraving. Image courtesy LooxisFL.com*

For a volumetric display that can come to life and change like video in realtime, we'll need to look at ways to turn colored light on and off for a volume of interest instead of simply having an image statically etched in place. A straightforward way to accomplish this is through the use of LEDs in a cube formation, wherein each single Light Emitting Diode acts as a voxel. Figure 9-2 shows such a device. It is built by eight-year-old Joey Hudy who is the driving force behind the site "Look What Joey's Making" at `http://lwjm.us/`. Joey builds the LED display shown in Figure 9-2 for sale. Visit his website to order yours today.

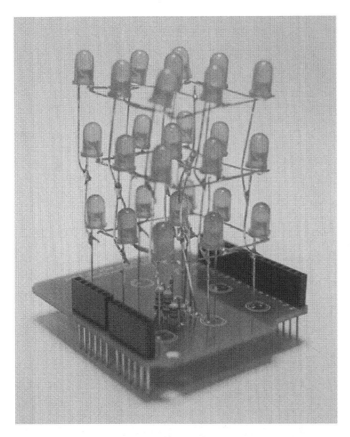

Figure 9-2. Arduino shield for a 3 × 3 × 3 LED display by eighth grader, Joey Hudy, courtesy of lwjm.us

One of the largest commercially available displays of this type has an array of 66×48×24 LED lights and is created by Seekway (http://seekway.com.cn). That's 76,032 individual lights that need to be wired up in a circuit and individually addressed with a microprocessor. The unit is roughly 6 feet tall, 1.5 feet deep and 3 feet wide. It costs many thousands of dollars.

▨ **Note** For the hobbyist who'd like to create their own simple LED display, two great resources are from articles at Instructables.com. One is for creating an 8×8 cube: `www.instructables.com/id/Led-Cube-8x8x8/` and the other is a bit simpler, for creating a 4×4×4 LED cube: `www.instructables.com/id/LED-Cube-4x4x4/`. And, of course, do not forget Joey Hudy's site at `http://lwjm.us/`.

Projection onto Static Volumes

A very clever technique to overcome the need to electrically wire up individual lights to a gridded out cube is to simply project light onto a reflective material at that volume of interest in space. Albert Hwang, Matt Parker, and Elliot Woods created Lumarca, an open source design project (Figure 9-3), to accomplish this through the hanging of hundreds of strings in a very special way so that a projector can be pointed into the mesh with extraordinary results. With custom software for calibration and very precise positioning of an SVGA (1024 × 768) projector into the string array, each string can be individually addressed with light, regardless of where it resides in space—at the front of the volume, at the back, and anywhere in between and side to side. Every string must be carefully placed so as not to obscure the projector beam from hitting another string behind it.

The details of how to construct one of these on your own for less than US$100 are on the project's website at http://madparker.com/lumarca/construction. At the New York MakerFaire 2011, the team debuted a pico projector- sized kit, roughly 1 foot cubed. Taking this miniaturization further, could "strings" or dots 3D laser etched into a small plastic prism with a pocket projector reproduce this type of display in a solid state medium? Researchers at Columbia have taken a step in this direction with their work on projected passive optical scattering (http://www.cs.columbia.edu/CAVE/projects/3d_display/). There's still much to research and develop with regard to volumetric 3D displays, so mixing and matching these techniques could lead to innovations previously undiscovered. Onward pioneers!

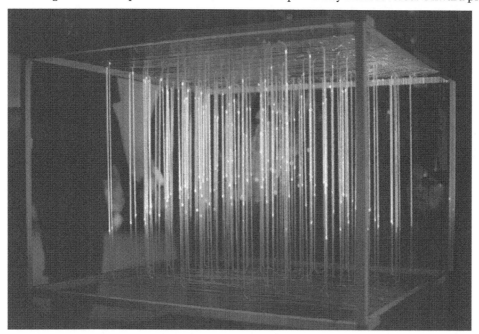

Figure 9-3. *Lumarca volumetric display with projection onto hanging strings. Photo by Jeff Howard*

Swept Volume Displays

Swept volume volumetric displays are in many ways the "traditional" volumetric display. Patent applications for these devices go back to the 1950s and 1960s but we only began to see actual implementation in the last couple of decades. A swept volume display takes a single light emitting 2D slice of a volume and, through a mechanism that rapidly moves the location of the slice and its content in context with the space it is pushing through, uses the persistence of vision optical effect to imprint a volumetric 3D image hanging in space.

In 1988, the New York Hall of Science spent US$40,000 to construct a volumetric 3D display that could interactively depict "The Quantum Atom." With the reciprocating mechanical motion of a platter painted with light from a computer controlled oscilloscope, the individual slices of a solid moving object were carved into space inside a cylinder, which allowed audiences to walk 360 degrees around the interactive electronic 3D image. Alan Jackson, the designer of that display, has launched a new initiative to get affordably-priced units that utilize the same reciprocating motion swept volume technique into the hands of developers, using modern hardware and open source software.

Alan's VoxieBox (http://voxiebox.com) will be available in kit or preassembled form starting in 2012. Similar to the OpenNI initiative of Primesense, the VoxieBox will promote an open source framework being developed for volumetric displays at OpenVoxel.org to attract a developer community that can take advantage of these devices' unique capabilities. While the Kinect has done so much to make technology accessibility for development around 3D capture, the VoxieBox and other devices that the OpenVoxel framework will support aspire to do the same for volumetric 3D displays. Unlike the proprietary commercial devices and research projects that debuted, and then failed to gather momentum in the public eye, efforts leveraging the passion of open source innovators have a chance for success.

One of those research projects was from the Institute for Creative Technologies at the University of Southern California. This project relied on a swept volume mechanism to enable their "Interactive 360º Light Field Display" (Figure 9-5). In this design, a projector is positioned pointing down from above the spinning mirror. This direct approach could be the basis for reproducing the desired effect in a controlled environment—perhaps an art, museum, or retail installation—for a more self-contained apparatus that doesn't have room for a projector at a distance. More information can be found about this system at http://gl.ict.usc.edu/Research/3DDisplay/.

In 2002, Actuality Systems introduced a product that used a swept volume technique similar to the rotating mirror system described by the Institute for Creative Technologies. Their device, Perspecta (Figure 9-4), cost roughly $30,000 and used a sophisticated series of optics under the rotating screen to make the device significantly more compact. Because the projection wasn't from above, a viewer could place their hand on top of the glass screen without interrupting the image display. Perspecta devices were marketed to the medical industry to visualize the volumetric imagery produced from MRI scanners. One drawback to systems that rely on physical motion to sweep out imagery is that parts can break down and need more frequent replacement than solid state systems and the persistence of vision effect can be interrupted from vibrations that disturb the intended path of the screen through space. Therefore, such systems would be unsuitable for mobile applications inside vehicles and unacceptable in environments exposed to the rumble of a spinning machine. Perhaps due to difficulty in gaining acceptance for such a unique product, Actuality Systems closed down in 2009 yet its engineers are available for consulting from opticsforhire.com.

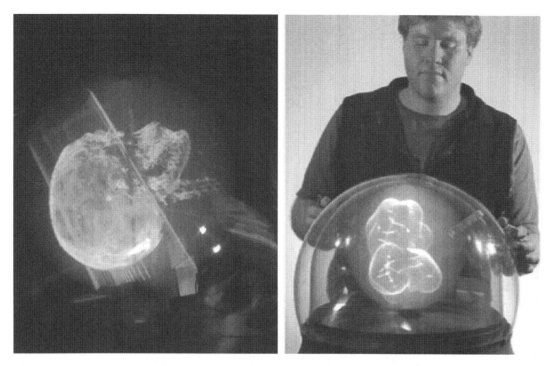

Figure 9-4. Perspecta Volumetric Display by Actuality Systems, Inc. Images courtesy OpticsForHire.com

One of the main drawbacks of these swept volume systems is the maintenance of the device with moving parts. LightSpace Technologies created a remarkable approach to address this problem with the DepthCube. By rapidly cycling a projected image onto one of 20 vertically stacked liquid crystal coated plates, a volume of slices that has depth is built up. The LCD plates remain opaque until electric current is applied, at which point they become transparent. Utilizing the DepthCube design, with only one of the 20 plates opaque at a time, a projector can present the correct image slice onto that plate from the full volume stack. With everything synced up and running very fast, persistence of vision blends the image slice stack into a cohesive volumetric image. See the DepthCube in action at http://youtu.be/RAasdH10Irg .

Other than in patent filings and academic papers, there is very little information online about how to construct your own swept volume display. This will change as more attention is drawn to their unique abilities. We need to see a greater community brought together with a shared interest in seeing this technology reach the mainstream. Until then, this how-to-guide for constructing a spinning swept volume with LED lights gives an idea of what is involved: http://bit.ly/makevolumedisplay.

Should you require a projector based image generator for high resolution displays where LED begins to show its limits, the DLP developer kits from Texas Instruments (http://bit.ly/dlpdevkits) provide a strong base to build upon. Texas Instruments' Digital Light Processing with a Digital Micromirror Device, which sells for $350, with the DLP Pico Projector Development Kit can run at 1,440 frames per second in one color, is smaller than a deck of cards, and produces an image brightness of 7 lumen, making it ideal for very short throw installations. At its native 480 × 320, you'll want to keep the projected image small to make for the densest image quality. For $3,500 the DLP LightCommander offers a more modular design—about the size of a fog machine—that can go up to 5,000 frames per second in monochrome binary pattern mode and supply 200 lumens-worth of light out of a Nikon f-mount interchangeable lens. Its native resolution is 1024 × 768. The DLP Discovery 4100 Kit costs upwards of US$8.000 and offers resolutions of HD 1080p (1920 ×1080), along with much more advanced feature sets.

Pepper's Ghost-Based Displays

While swept volume techniques can produce true volumetric 3D imagery that hangs in the air, providinga unique perspective from every angle, the price tag for such systems are prohibitively high, especially for displays that are relatively small. On the other end of the spectrum and dating back to the 1860s, is a technique that was developed as a theatrical special effect, which can scale to very large environments and which has been used to provide a convincing "in air" visual effect. John Henry Pepper's illusion was originally used to magically display transparent ghosts on stage for a performance of Charles Dickens's *A Haunted Man*. Now referred to as "Pepper's Ghost" (Figure 9-5), this optical illusion relies on the reflection of light from an obscured source onto a transparent film or glass plate where the image is seen to be hanging in space. This same principle is what makes teleprompters and heads-up displays work. Variations on this technique are behind many "holographic" imagery effects and displays.

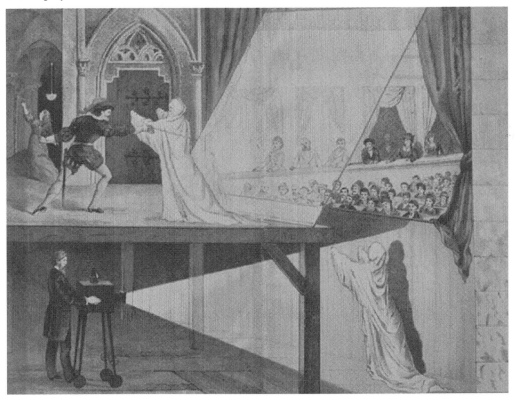

Figure 9-5. Illustration of the "Pepper's Ghost" illusion by Professor John Henry Pepper at London's Royal Polytechnic, 1881

A number of commercial solutions are available to bring this type of display to life on both large and small scales. Musion Eyeliner 3D (http://eyeliner3d.com) and Arena 3D Industrial Illusion (http://arena3d.com) sell and lease systems that are used for trade exhibits and major entertainment productions. Teleportec (www.teleportec.com/) sells a smaller system tailored to telepresence, which can place a remotely conferenced person behind a podium for a speech or at a board table for a meeting.

Alexander McQueen received much fanfare for his use of a Pepper's Ghost-based illusion for his *Widows of Culloden*, autumn/winter 2006/2007 fashion show, in which Kate Moss materialized and floated above the stage. Prerecorded video of the model, shot from four different angles, 90 degrees apart, was reflected from hidden screens suspended above four panels of glass that formed a transparent pyramid shape.

▦ **Note** Illustrated characters from the band Gorillaz famously performed live at the 2007 Grammy awards with Madonna via the Eyeliner 3D system; however, because the thin film used to reflect off of it is sensitive to vibrations, it is less than ideal for a thunderously loud concert setting. The band has since discontinued use of "holographic" stage tricks.

A number of companies have created smaller self-contained Pepper's Ghost-based display cases that work well for showcasing a hovering or transparent product—even mixing digital video and a real physical object into the same display area. Figure 9-6 shows a simple three-sided Pepper's Ghost design using a MacBook. This design was created by Ujjval Panchal. You can read more at his blog: http://blog.ujjvalpanchal.com/3d-holographic-display-prototype-1/.

Figure 9-6. Three-pane Pepper's Ghost display with MacBook. Photo courtesy Ujjval Panchal

HoloCube (www.holocube.eu/) has a number of simple and pleasing box-shaped designs for viewing in one direction. RealFiction (www.realfiction.com/) and Vizoo (www.vizoo.com/) sell pyramid-shaped systems, working off an arrangement similar to the Alexander McQueen show, that allow viewing from 180 to 360 degrees with either three or four separate channels of video corresponding to different angles.

▧ **Note** Because the imagery being presented on these displays originates from 2D screens or projection sources, they are not truly volumetric or "holographic" in the sense that you can look around objects from any angle.

An innovative use of the Pepper's Ghost technique is to separate a single 2D display or projection into multiple Pepper's Ghost layers, which can be stacked up to recreate a foreground, middle ground, and background. A prototype accessory for the iPhone was created on this principle, called i3dg (Figure 9-7), and at lost word was slated to go into production early in 2012. You can see the display in action in this video—http://youtu.be/JnGPtVNmtvI—and learn more at http://i3dg.mobi.

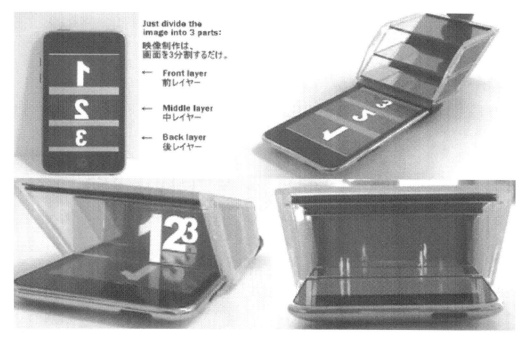

Figure 9-7. The i3Dg accessory for iPhone utilizes three panes of plastic to create a multi-depth experience, utilizing the principle of Pepper's Ghost. Image courtesy i3Dg

The original mock-up for this design came from using plastic CD cases; others online have successfully recreated this effect using various materials. On a larger scale, with a flatscreen TV or uniquely shaped projection surface, this technique could be employed to create a very eye-catching experience with a real sense of depth and motion parallax with the right content or application.

Multi View Autostereoscopic Flatscreens

Of all the technologies described in this chapter, multiview autostereoscopic displays are the most mature and accessible technology. Available from a variety of specialized providers, they can be used with existing development tools at a cost that is not as prohibitive as the more researched and industrial level technologies. The market size is currently about 2–4 thousand autostereoscopic 3D displays per year for digital signage applications, which keeps the price tag for these items around US$5,000. Each display requires a significant amount of resources to carefully produce—from custom manufacturing precision slanted lenticular sheets for every model of LCD to the "clean room" environment needed to adhere the multiview layer to the screen. Additionally, the custom content production and hardware requirements can be substantial for delivering enough views to the screens to make the viewing experience truly eye popping without causing eye strain. Mainstream consumer adoption of such screens would drive the cost down considerably—just as Kinect did for the depth-sensing volumetric camera market.

Displays are available from a variety of manufacturers. Magnetic3D (http://magnetic3d.com), 3DFusion (http://3dfusion.com), and Exceptional3D (http://exceptional3d.com) are all based in New York and offer nine-view displays at varying levels of size and quality. Alioscopy (http://alioscopyusa.com / http://alioscopy.com), uses an eight-view display technique. Lower-end displays can be found with four and five views, and on the high end, Dimenco (www.dimenco.eu), founded by a team that worked on autostereoscopic screens at Philips, boasts a twenty-eight-view system. Dimenco's approach relies on 2D + depth map source material and a dedicated hardware "rendering box," which limits its potential to use native multiview content. Magnetic3D's nine-view allows a center channel to act as a reference image with four views to each the left and right for peering around an object. In a slated lenticular design, finding the right compromise between the number of views to give a good motion parallax and not packing so many views in that there is ghosting or cross-talk between the layers of pixels underneath is a careful balance.

As with any of the volumetric displays discussed in this chapter, somewhere along the line, you'll have to figure out how you will optimize multiple views of your application or content to match the physical properties of a display. These screens are at their best when the viewer can feel depth that both drops behind the screen and protrudes out from it. Thomas J. Zerega, founder of Magnetic3D, suggests that content and application developers can design experiences that utilize these displays to their limits, enabling "True Volumetric Perception" by following best practices in how content is prepared. When visual assets protruding out from the plane of the screen get cut off by the LCD's border edges, a "window violation" that disturbs the perception of depth is produced. To avoid this experience, programmers can create in-app physics that avoid such glitches by design. You can use this effect to your advantage by letterboxing the display area; that is, placing a black border around the content on the screen. This way, when an object is meant to come out from the screen, it can break the digital letterboxing—to a great popping effect—without getting cut off by the hard physical "boxing" of the display edge.

Laser Plasma Emission Displays

If the idea of producing images hanging in air instead of stuck to a screen is what you are after—pulsed laser's crackling light in free space is going to excite you. Japan's National Institute of Advanced Industrial Science and Technology (http://bit.ly/plasmaemission) has partnered with Keio University and Burton Inc. to push the edge of using lasers to light up air molecules in a true volumetric display that works without the need for a generated medium such as mist.

The mechanism by which this type of display works is fascinating on two levels. First, it shows a real time demonstration of a dynamic display that matches the variable point abilities of the static plastic etching laser noted at the beginning of thischapter. This is great, because the mechanism isn't bound by a set grid of voxels that it must adhere to. This is in contrast to other static or swept displays, which are locked into the boundaries of pixels or LEDs.

The second level of interest is the inspiration to apply the optical tricks leveraged to focus the laser beam to other types of display optics. The use of a diffusion lens moving in the z-axis and a second optic modulating in the x and y plane might have application with the other approaches outlined in this chapter. As more interest gravitates towards the aspiration of true volumetric displays, we're bound to see a mixing and matching of these techniques to bring about more breakthroughs. Stay tuned to Burton, Inc (http://burton-jp.com) for more developments with this technology. The latest demonstration of their display can show 50,000 voxel points in space per second. Check out the videos at http://youtu.be/EndNwMBEiVU and http://youtu.be/KfVS-npfVuY to see it in action.

Free-space Aerosol Displays

Molecules that float in air—sprayed water, dense fog, and fine mist—can be used as a medium for projection with stunning results. The commercial products that fall into this category tend to be based on 2D source material, so their degree of true volumetricness is owing to the illusion that a borderless volume of space contains a floating slice of imagery without the traditional boundaries of a screen. However, in custom engineered setups with multiple sources of imagery and clever manipulations of in-air particles, anything is possible.

■ **Note** You can view an excellent image from "In the Evening at Koi Pond" at:

`http://commons.wikimedia.org/wiki/File:In_the_Evening_at_Koi_Pond_in_Expo_2005.JPG`.

The market for this type of display is often stage shows or big events with an array of unique lighting of which an in-air display is one part of the larger experience. At the World's Fair EXPO 2005 in Japan, I witnessed a remarkable use of this technique in Robert Wilson's "In the Evening at Koi Pond". This system combined projections on giant solid objects floating in a pond with multiple projections in fountain mist that floated hundreds of feet in the air. The use of free space projection was reserved for moments when a certain character would appear or other accents to the main choreography took place. This gave those moments jaw-dropping impact.Therefore in an installation or performance situation, consider theuse of the techniques described in this chapter in combination for best effect.

The IO2 Heliodisplay

The IO2 Heliodisplay (www.io2technology.com) uses ambient air passed through a series of thermal controlled metal plates to create a sheet of ultrafine invisible articles that jet out from the unit. At less than 10 microns, the semi-invisible atomized water particles are similar to human breath when exhaled. Therefore, there is no visible fog or heavy moisture from this unique design in contrast to other approaches. Used in combination with a high-powered 4500 lumen projector, optimized for a rear projection setup and this air stream, a visible image can be seen to hang in the air a distance from the unit (Figure 9-8). The unit costsUS $48,000 forthe base model, and US$68,000 for an interactive unit.

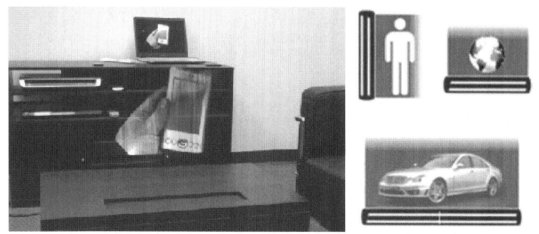

Figure 9-8. *Heliodisplay embedded in a table and various orientation options. Image i2o Technologies*

An upright configuration, which can be hidden in a wall, casts the air stream out horizontally and can be tall enough to project an image of a life-sized human. A table-mounted unit sends the air stream up vertically with the effect of an image floating above the surface. The unit can also be hung upside down and send the screen out in virtually any direction on special order. The trick is to design content with a black background and hide all of the physical components, as well as the projector and the heliodisplay unit, so all that is seen is the floating imagery. The system does not work with a front projection or short throw projector, so you'll need to configure this in such a way that you can place the projector about five feet behind it. A small tank filled with tap water allows the unit to run for a couple of days to a week, depending on its settings; a special disk needs to be replaced every sixmonths to a year. It can even be used outdoors—but you'll need an environment without too much wind, as windwill distort the image. Speaking of distortion, don't expect this to look as clear and crisp as a flatscreen normal projection TV. If you look closely at the product images, you can see that a streaking effect is noticeable. As with any technology, it's best to consider how to leverage limitations in a way that makes them look like advantages, perhaps working the streaks and wavy flow of the screen into an aesthetic that fits the application.

The FogScreen Display

If you don't need something up close and personal, and instead want to go larger than life for the stage—look no further than the FogScreen (fogscreen.com) from Finland (Figure 9-9). Their units use a laminar airflow process to create a thin screen made of water in the form of visible fog, and ultrasonic waves. Their entry-level unit, the FogScreen EZ, is priced under US $30,000 and unlike the Heliodisplay, is available to rent worldwide. The FogScreen Pro can be connected in series for variable scale installations and is available for order by the meter starting at US $33,000 for one meter, US $100,000 for four meters, and US $175,000 for eight meters, with a variety of prices in between.

Figure 9-9. *FogScreen projections at E3 conference.* Photo by wili_hybrid.

The FogScreen gets a great deal of use in stage lighting and event displays, whereas the i2o unit is more suited for intimate settings at a smaller scale. In contrast to the floor- and wall-mounted Heliodisplay, the Fogscreen works in one orientation—from above. This allows the unit to be hidden out of the way along with its projector attached to the ceiling. Because the light scatters rather than reflects from the particles in the air, the FogScreen must also be used in a rear projection capacity. This property could be used to your advantage, as some researchers have experimented with two projectors pointing at either side of the screen to show a different image, giving a sense of 3D. The FogScreen has controls to change the level of opacity in the screen. That means you can use it for a "reveal" effect of someone coming out from behind a curtain of projection, or make it transparent enough to appear floating in air with no edges.

One especially promising technique relies on the fact that dispersion of light through fog has directionality. At the Interaction 2011 conference, researchers from Osaka University used a three-projector setup pointed at a cylinder of fog to demonstrate different images of a 3D object based on different angles of view, satisfying motion parallax. Remarkable video of this innovative technique can be seen at http://youtu.be/yzIeiyzRLCw. The use of multiple projectors to satisfy multiple views into a scene is the basis for light field-based displays.

Projected Light Field Arrays

An area of volumetric imaging currently receiving much attention relates to the use of an array of projectors to recreate multiple views of a scene onto a diffused light filter. The general idea is that, the more projectors you can add at more angles, the better you can recreate the original light field of a 3D scene. Therefore, when the viewer observes the scene through a special diffuser film, the movement of the viewer's head through the viewing angle will stimulate the motion parallax required to provide the sensation of viewing a 3D scene. With the advent of low cost projectors, including pico class devices of diminutive size, this approach is much more financially feasible then it would have been only a few years ago.

The projected light field approach is applied to produce a novel effect in fVisiOn—floating 3D vision on the table—a research project from Shunsuke Yoshida at Japan's National Institute of Information and Communications Technology. The intent of this project is to create a display that doesn't interfere with the workspace of a table, but instead allows for the comingling of real 3D objects and virtual ones.

▓ **Note** You can learn more and watch a video at the project's website:

http://mmc.nict.go.jp/people/shun/fVisiOn/fVisiOn.html.

Instead of implementing a standard planar sheet to combine the projected light into a cohesive 3D image, the fVisiOn approach relies on a cone shaped screen. As seen in Figure 9-10, the display is made up of an array of pico projectors all pointed inward in a circle onto the cone. The white dots of light visible in the upper right hand image show the densely packed ring of projectors. Two layers of filtered material are placed on top of the cone to increase the contrast in the image.

Figure 9-10. *The fVisiOn display deconstructed. Upper left shows the cone shaped diffuser and pico projector at one angle; upper right shows dozens of projectors in place, appearing as dots of light; lower left and right show two layers of filters that increase the contrast in the image to produce a floating digital object.*

While the fVisiOn provides insight into how light field displays can be used on a small scale, many are eager to know how volumetric 3D experiences will scale up to bring voxies to the big screen of a theatre. The answers may lie in a series of innovation initiatives spearheaded by the European Union. Three projects: HOLOVISION (www.holovisionproject.org), OSIRIS (www.osiris-project.eu), and COHERENT (www.coherentproject.org) were established to position European countries and companies as the leading pioneers of holographic media capture, transmission, and display. The primary integrator for these technologies is a Hungarian company called Holographika (www.holografika.com/).

Through the use of roughly 100 projectors focused on a diffusion screen, Holographika's displays recreate a light field to provide a discreet view into a scene, dependent on each viewer's position with regard to the screen. This technique is similar to the efforts from Osaka University researchers with fog, the difference being, this company now has units in production ready to be rented or purchased. It's fitting that a Hungarian company achieved this marvel, as it was, in fact, a Hungarian scientist who invented the field of holography.

While the products from Holographika are not priced for consumers, ranging from US $45,000–150,000, they've set the bar very high and will provide a reference spec by which to judge future solutions. For home and office usage, the rear projection models appear visually similar to early widescreen TVs before plasma and LCD. In order to pack all the projectors inside, there needs to be enough depth to bounce the images onto the screen. However, the more breathtaking innovation lies in the front projected solution for large scale theatre environments(Figure 9-11).

Figure 9-11. HoloVizio C80 by Holografika

The HoloVizio C80 has ushered in the age of volumetric 3D movie theatres, what people may one day call the voxies for short. This isn't science fiction. The C80 unit is currently being demonstrated in trade shows around the world. Where traditional movie theatres have one projector, or perhaps two for stereoscopic 3D, Holographika's technique employs upwards of 80 projectors. Presently, the maximum-sized screen is around 140" wide—large enough for a small indie theatre. Now, we just need a new generation of storytellers to kick start the voxie business with volumetric motion pictures that take advantage of this disruptive innovation. Which would you pay more for—a night out at the movies or the voxies?

CHAPTER 10

Where Do We Go From Here?

Working on this book has meant a lot to each of us. In the Kinect, we see a wonderful device that can be used for creative expression. We also see a device and technology that is capable of changing the way we put technology to work in our daily lives. At first, the Kinect and its skeleton-tracking technology are all about games and cool art projects. But it doesn't end there. The underlying technology has profound implications on how people and technology interact. In this Afterword, we each offer a few final thoughts on the impact of the technology and where it might take us in the future.

Sean Kean

I hope this introduction to development with the Microsoft Kinect has provided you with a solid foundation from which to execute new ideas that redefine our relationship with technology. You now have the building blocks for creating experiences that can help us move past the limited means of interacting with machines from the past and pave the way to a more humane relationship between people and devices in the future. As someone who initially became interested in technology for artistic and social expression, I've always felt the mouse and keyboard were a legacy of office environments that fell short of capturing the ways I wanted to play with machines. Innovations such as the Kinect, as well as the software that you will now go forth and develop, will write a new chapter of how society and technology evolve with one another.

Roughly one year after the Kinect's debut in November 2010, we've seen this device put to use in so many breathtaking ways. It's been overwhelming to keep track of or even classify the different usages. Seeing the public's imagination captured by the 'Kinect hacks' that have flooded the web, it's clear that body gesture-based control of software is something people are eager to have integrated into their lifestyle once they've witnessed it. However, one application of this technology hasn't received quite as much attention as the others and it's the one I've been most excited about since I first saw Oliver Kreyos demonstrate it in a post to YouTube last year.

In a video entitled "3D Video Capture with Kinect" (http://youtube/7QrnwoO1-8A), posted just ten days after the device hit stores, Oliver was the first to show volumetric 3D video that allows a viewer to move a virtual camera 360 degrees around a live scene during its recording. This still blows my mind and I think it's the sleeping giant of the Kinect that will mark a fundamental shift in the way motion pictures, photography, and live video will be experienced in the very near future. Once the tools for creating, sharing, and viewing volumetric 3D video can be demonstrated in a more mature state for the general population to consider, I'm confident that we will see widespread adoption of it for everything from video conferencing to sports, to feature films and truly 3D game systems. This is the dawning of the volumetric age.

I have feared for some time that with so much exposure to flat screen media on televisions, computers, and phones, society has eroded some of our innate abilities to decode the physical 3D world around us. I believe this shift from 2D to volumetric 3D experiences has the potential to reignite hope for a new spatial awareness that can revive a section of our minds that has lain dormant since screen media became ubiquitous. Things will truly get interesting once digital media can more closely match the depth perception capabilities we were born with but have had no way to reconcile with 2D media and traditional software interfaces.

Let's take a look at what's involved in bringing about the volumetric 3D video revolution. By examining how 2D video is created and experienced by consumers today, we can look at what needs to be put in place to do the same for volumetric 3D. Along the way, I hope you see a number of exciting opportunities to develop technology that fits into the needs that will arise as creators go from shooting 2D motion pictures to pioneering the voxies, video that is viewable from any 360 degree angle and is based on the voxel point cloud imagery generated from devices such as the Kinect.

For a consumer, recording HD video with an iPhone, trimming it on the device, and uploading it to YouTube or Facebook to share with the world is remarkably effortless. A professional may choose to use a more elaborate SLR camera that would require the additional step of connecting it to a computer along with opting to edit the video in a program, such as FinalCut or iMovie, before uploading it to the web, perhaps opting for an alternative video sharing site such as Vimeo.com. Refined over many years, there are simple, affordable, and accessible solutions for users to capture, edit, and view shared video. We will need comparable devices, services, and software to bring volumetric 3D to the mainstream market. Luckily, millions of people now have a device to capture basic volumetric 3D video with the Kinect.

If you followed through till the end of chapter 1, you've already seen yourself captured in primitive volumetric 3D and are able to spin around your view with a synthetic camera. The latest versions of Microsoft's SDK, as well as OpenNI, lets developers make use of multiple Kinects that could be arranged in such a way to fill in the empty shadows resulting from just one camera. With the KinectFusion project, Microsoft Research shows us that there is a bright future ahead for reconstructing full 3D models of scenes in realtime (see Figure 1-25) using just one Kinect and software utilizing standard computer graphics processing chipsets. The only problem with the Kinect as a video recording device is that the user is tethered to a computer and wall outlet. This has resulted in Kinect videos containing roughly the same subject matter – people sitting at their computers.

I'd much rather shoot active video running around outdoors, adventuring in remote locations, and everything else we've come to expect that is possible from portable electronics today. Prior to the introduction of Sony's Portapak in 1967, video was pretty much immobile – just as we are today with the Kinect. TV studio equipment was so large and power intensive that it had to stay in the studio. After the Portapak's introduction, video art flourished with artists such as Nam June Paik and Bill Viola, who strapped on battery powered equipment and used the medium to explore visual expression in ways that were previously only available by working with film. Today, every smartphone is far more capable than a Portapak – yet we will likely want to return to specialty hardware devices to take advantage of volumetric 3D's promise. This will create exciting opportunities for those that wish to design and manufacture novel cinematic tools.

For higher production quality capture, there is an exciting array of possiblities that go beyond the Kinect. The structured light approach from the PrimeSense solution is not able to work outside in bright lighting conditions that interfere with the infrared laser. Time-of-flight sensors offer one alternative to go where the Kinect cannot; however, their depthmap resolution is currently much smaller than that which is offered by PrimeSense and still relies on emitted light with a limited sensing range. A remarkable new imagining technology called a light field, or plenoptic, camera debuted this year from Lytro (www.lytro.com) that may eventually be embedded into a tool for the volumetric cinematographer.

This unique imager makes use of a micro lens array that computes all the light rays entering the camera from a number of angles and produces a depthmap similar to 3D sensors such as the Kinect. While not yet a realtime video solution, keep your eye on how this technology develops. An array of Lytro cameras surrounding a scene from different angles would not only be able to gather multiple depthmaps without interference from each other, but they would also be able to refocus on any point in an scene at the time of viewing. This would result in the type of depth of field that we've come to expect from high quality SLR cameras, but conceivably in realtime based on the users's perspective into an image. Lytro's consumer focused product may turn out to be just as disruptive and accessible to hack as the Kinect. Its breakthrough price point of US$399 is astonishing when you consider Raytrix's (http://raytrix.de) cameras, the only competitor, start at around US$20,000.

Before the Kinect, there was a lot of research into techniques for computing 3D scene information from stereo cameras and multi camera arrays in a technique called photogrammetry. With the advent of more mature cloud computing environments, a number of solutions are cropping up to handle this type of image processing on remote servers to reduce the requirements on user machines. Processing still imagery from an array of cameras at different perspectives is now possible using tools such as Autodesk's 123D Catch (http://123dapp.com/catch) and Hypr3D (www.hypr3d.com) with photomapped 3D models of a scene returned after uploading a series of images. For use on your local machine, AgiSoft's PhotoScan (http://www.agisoft.ru/) is a desktop photogrammetry solution available for Windows and Mac OS X. By using a number of inexpensive HD cameras, such as those available from GoPro (www.gopro.com), its conceivable to assemble a large rig with dozens of units that would capture video from an assortment of angles and then break down each frame from each camera into a series of photogrammetry batch processing jobs. Combined with 3D sensors, such as the Kinect to aid in depth mapping, we are bound to see some very interesting solutions for generating high quality volumetric 3D imagery with a blend of these techniques.

What's the difference between producing a movie in 2D and a voxie in volumetric 3D? To start, movie directors are accustomed to having absolute control over the viewer's perspective into a story through a single camera view. However, in the world of the voxie, the budding volumetric cinematographer must wrestle with choreographing performers, lighting, and camera rigs during production in a way that takes into account the way that the audience may gaze into the scene from any angle, such as by moving their head, using a controller, or simply walking around a volumetric display. But that's only the start. We'll need entirely new software to handle post production editing, transmission, storage, and display of this truly new media.

The good news is this software is being actively developed right now. The first live internet video stream of volumetric 3D video occurred during the Art&&Code 3D (http://artandcode.com/3d) event in Pittsburg in October 2011. This transmitted a 360 degree video of the speakers straight to web browsers tuning in around the world. This marked a significant technical accomplishment that will no doubt begin to inspire others to create more robust solutions that move beyond the limitations of sharing this depth-enabled media on systems such as YouTube and Vimeo, which currently have no capacity to store the complete volumetric data in their 2D file format.

A YouTube for volumetric 3D video, or free viewpoint video (FVV) as it is also refereed, could act as a repository for large voxel datasets in video form that could be analyzed and reprocessed with more sophisticated algorithms for 3D reconstruction, such as KinectFusion when they become available at a later point. Many people may choose to upload all of their raw volumetric video to the cloud and use web-based editing services to finish their videos in order to minimize the processing requirements on their own equipment. For more sophisticated directors, there will be a demand for professional grade workstation software for local editing and post production effects. Back in the cloud, machine vision middleware, similar to Primesense's NITE, could provide novel features based on user segmenting, skeletal tracking, and pattern recognition that could be applied to uploads in order to generate structured information for categorizing videos, objects within them, and even the semantic analysis of storylines. Once the videos are online with interactive and embeddable viewers, we can expect to see them shared online within Facebook streams and linked into the same places where 2D photos and video are used now. The opportunity for users to create mashups and remixes of user submitted volumetric video will be fascinating to watch unfold as clever artists and programmers leverage the capabilities of depth-enabled video in ways that are hard to predict.

Yet there isn't much use in capturing volumetric video if you are just going to look at it on a plain old 2D screen. While interim solutions will be available that use head tracking to allow you to experience simulated motion parallax to look around volumetric 3D on 2D screens, the driving reason to develop this type of content will result from the availability of true volumetric 3D displays that mature from techniques documented in chapter 9. As more compelling voxel-based video content and services are created, along with games and professional 3D applications, volumetric displays will break through a whole new era of entertainment and spatial computing. As recently demonstrated by Microsoft Research's work with a touch interface for both a true 360 degree volumetric 3D display called Vermeer (http://research.microsoft.com/en-us/projects/vermeer/) and a their Holodesk (http://research.microsoft.com/apps/video/default.aspx?id=154571), which relies on head tracking, interacting with touchable imagery that occupies real 3D space opens up a realm of opportunities that were previously considered science fiction.

What kind of content and applications will consumers desire when the ability to reach out and touch volumetric video displays is priced within reach? We'll soon find out and that's where I'll be going from here. Join the volumetric age by getting involved in the community at volumetric.org and by following updates to this book at meetthekinect.com .

--Sean Kean

Phoenix Perry

Sages of the future often look foolish in hindsight. Frequently, they overstate the speed of immediate developments and underestimate the huge changes coming in the long term. That said, I am writing this prediction on the day of the death of Steve Jobs. The era of mouse-based computing has come to a close. The doors of Apple stores across America are covered in candles and the playing field for the future of computing is wide open. Gesture based computing is the future of interface design. This revolution has been developing for 20 years and the time for it is finally here. Visual recognition systems, touch screens, gesture based interfaces and voice control will be combined to replace remotes and mice over the next 5 years, particularly in casual computing experiences. User experiences will become more organic and biocentric. The wave of natural interfaces is the next big boom coming in design technology.

My disenchantment with the mouse began in 1999 when I developed an extreme case of carpel tunnel. The interface of my personal computer broke my body through bad design. I couldn't comb my hair. My boyfriend brushed my teeth and the tool that had allowed me to become a thriving creator had destroyed my body. As a result, I've spent the last 10 years healing and exploring alternate modes for computer control that allow for long term use without harming the human body. With these new modes of interactivity, we can safely develop computing experiences that match our bodies and work for the span of a human lifetime. The computing experience is being wildly rethought. Designers and DIY makers are pushing the market forward by creating new experiences. Users hunger for richer, more personalized, tactile experiences. We are rethinking the digital experience and integrating it into the human experience. From reactive signage integrating facial recognition with mobile shopping experiences and smart living rooms to new ways to heal the mind and body, there is no end to the immersive experiences waiting to be created.

Culturally, music and art making are being torn wide open. Your instrument can be anything you could possibly imagine and even draw with your fingers in the air. Media artists can map video and images directly on the body, including the face, with precision. Motion capture can happen in your living room. Artists can draw in 3D in the physical world with just their hands and then print the results out via a desktop fabrication machine bought for under $3000 from MakerBot Industries. Research is being done with brain wave control that might allow artists to work by simply closing their eyes. The future has arrived. It just looks different than we expected, and fortunately it's not the pristine corporate modeled plastic interface of the past but seamlessly integrating into the human landscape. The future of design is open source and in the hands of the makers.

--Phoenix Perry

Johnathan C. Hall

If you're reading this, I can assume that you at least find Microsoft's Kinect and other Kinect-like sensors to be intriguing. If you were born in the last millennium and don't take every technological feat for granted, you might even agree that these devices are pretty amazing. But are they revolutionary? I don't have the answer, but I can tell you where I'm looking for this technology to support social, cultural, and economic change—for better and worse—and it's not in the living room. It's in public and quasi-public spaces.

A touch-free computer interface has a certain utility that's inherent in its touchlessness. For example, a touch-free interface is more hygienic and therefore offers clear advantages if used in hospitals and doctor's offices, in clean rooms, operating rooms, and rest rooms. A touch-free interface can also empower even vertically-challenged people like me (I'm 5'9"... okay 5'8"... on my tippy toes) to intuitively manipulate arbitrarily large media for experiences in immersive entertainment, art, education, or marketing. A touch-free interface can even initiate "passive" interaction by responding to where and how many people are situated in a given space and providing intelligent, contextual feedback. much like the "ubiquitous computing" scenarios envisioned by the legendary Xerox PARC scientist Mark Weiser among others.

There remain, of course, significant barriers to our realization of these benefits. For example, I was mortified by my very first Kinect experience when, after a vigorous round of Kinect Adventures, I was presented with pictures of myself caught in compromising poses. As my Xbox threatened to post them to Facebook. I shrieked, "Noooooooooo!" and dove to yank the plug out of the wall. Who's going to be caught dead gesticulating like a moron anywhere *but* their living room?

Ten years ago, I might've asked, equally incredulous, "Who's going to be caught dead having a messy breakup with their significant other over the phone on a crowded train?" And yet, this genre is a staple in the soundtrack of commuter life in major metropolitan areas. The point is our cultural rules and habits do change in the wake of technological innovation and adoption: witness the mobile phone.

I believe that people will grow accustomed to a certain constrained repertoire of motion-controlled interactions with public screens over time. Part of that evolution is cultural, but part of it is in the technology itself or, more specifically, in the design of applications. Applications for touch-free interfaces in public spaces will necessarily be less physically demanding than Kinect Adventures or most Xbox games, and will be more like the Xbox dashboard, intended for quick, casual, mostly utilitarian interaction. My work on Sensecast (see Chapter 3) is designed to support just this level of engagement: check in for a meeting in the lobby, browse some information relevant to your health at the doctor's office, grab the full text of a news story on your phone, and go. (Of course, it's far too early in the lifecycle of this work to say that we are doing it right.)

Like our willingness to post our "status" publicly on Facebook or to "check in" at a Starbucks, our interactions with public screens have the potential to create whole new ecosystems of cultural and economic value, as well as exploitation, as we'll see below. My hope is that we can steer this potential toward the good: to transform public spaces into more sociable places through shared media that orchestrates our interaction not only with computers but with each other. Our collective habit today is one of passive, solitary media consumption. Smart filters, niche blogs, and micro-blogging let us tailor our media diets to only our own interests. So-called social and mobile apps, meanwhile, isolate us from our geographic communities by channeling our attention away from them. Imagine Kinected applications that get us on our feet in common spaces, meeting our neighbors, permeating our day-to-day lives. Imagine:

- 8:00 a.m. On the train platform, commuters gather around a display that bears headlines and photos from a town council meeting the night before. One reads: "Youth Center to Go to Referendum." The display polls the surrounding audience for a literal thumbs-up or thumbs-down on this decision, records their gestures, and collects/displays the aggregate town sentiment. Before you board the train, you can beam the full story to your mobile phone.

- 3:00 p.m. High school student council members meet in the public arcade with signs urging action on the town's stalled youth center project. They hold the signs up to a community display, where an onboard Kinect recognizes their activity and snaps a photo, distributing the image across a town-wide network.

- 7:00 p.m. A chime sounds in a crowded café, and a ceiling-mounted digital display starts showing quiz questions about local data: Did the crime rate go up or down this year? What percent of the town budget goes to education? How much does the average family pay in property taxes? Onlookers are able to "buzz in" by mimicking a game-show push-button with two hands. The display then selects and follows whomever buzzed in first, allowing him/her to choose an answer on screen.

While I've given my examples a decidedly civic cast to make a point, a much broader set of applications and games will no doubt be unleashed upon our public spaces by creative technology companies, advertisers, non-profits, and government entities in the years to come. Some will be good and some bad. But the potential is there is to create real value for people by delivering rich experiences, critical information, and spontaneous play around the shared interests and spaces of real, not virtual, communities. By designing for public and quasi-public spaces, developers of Kinected applications can explore a new era of real, not virtual, social and location-based media.

The first application for Sensecast was a news browser placed just outside a Columbia Journalism School café in a semi-public building with high foot traffic. It encouraged passers-by to read a given story lede, and if so moved, to "like" it with a thumbs-up gesture. Why? Our historian colleagues at the J School note that before 1900, people didn't read newspapers alone but rather aloud with friends and strangers gathered around. If philosopher Jürgen Habermas is to be believed, this socio-political dimension of public life, now lost to history, can support a more vital democracy. Perhaps with shared, Kinected news displays that persuade us to also connect with each other, we can resuscitate it.

Maybe. But maybe not. Privacy is a holy term in the American and European lexicons and publicity a suspect one (consider the words "publicity stunt," "publicity whore," etc.). The humanist geographer Yi-Fu Tuan points out that, in the ancient Greek world, these poles were reversed: privacy is related to the Greek word for idiot, as purely private folk were considered to be like shut-ins not fit for any role in society. Meanwhile, the lofty peaks of human flourishing were reserved for those willing to roll out to the agora, to make themselves known, to act on a public stage. In most of the modern world, however, privacy is king.

Still, the jury on publicity is not yet in. We tack between obliviousness to the tools of surveillance (security cameras, browser cookies, social networks, etc.) and a justified paranoia about them. As I wax euphoric about the potential of Kinect-like cameras to transform public space for the better, no doubt some of you are growing duly uncomfortable with the level of surveillance that's entailed—or, at least, enabled.

I consider these concerns, as I've said, "justified paranoias." While I freely refer to the Kinect as a "camera," you will note that Microsoft and device manufacturers in the space explicitly do not. They diligently assert their preferred term: "sensor." That choice is a conscious marketing decision intended to make vague the data that the device collects. As you've seen throughout this book, these "sensors" that we've willingly invited into our homes are powerful cameras capable of passively collecting quite a bit of intimate detail about us, our dimensions, our homes, and our families. We know from patent filings that as Microsoft rolls out live TV service on its Xbox platform—replacing cable's set-top box—the company is integrating Kinect into systems for parental control and advertising. The Kinect not only provides you a convenient remote control that you will never lose again, it provides Microsoft and its partners a rich profile of you and realtime data on who's watching. We're all Nielsen families now!

This all may seem creepy. Do we just accept as true the dystopian aphorism promulgated by Napster creator Sean Parker in a recent talk at the 2011 Web 2.0 Summit in San Francisco–"Today's creepy is tomorrow's necessity"?

Again, I don't have the answer. I've chosen to focus my work on Kinected applications for public spaces, a domain that *seems* less frought with privacy concerns than whatever the likes of Microsoft, Apple, Google, and Facebook might be doing with our "private" data. This domain is not free of concern, of course. Consider that 3D-hinted facial recognition algorithms are probably an order of magnitude more robust than their straight 2D counterparts. Deploying Kinects widely in public space could conceivably spell the end to anonymity in public. Of course, that outcome is a ways off and possibly intractable, as ownership of physical space is not nearly as consolidated as ownership of, say, mobile platforms, thus preventing any one party from owning all the data. But is it technologically possible? Yes.

In any case, there is clearly a non-trivial trade-off to be made when weighing the values of privacy and publicity. Companies and individuals have built amazing products and made them available to us for free or at low cost in exchange for a share of our privacy. And indeed, like the ancient Greeks, we may stand to gain something ourselves by living more public lives. We also stand to be exploited and sold as "eyeballs," or now "skeletons." No doubt the Kinect and the ecosystem of companies and developers building with it will stretch concepts of privacy and publicity in new directions. You, by picking up this book and doing with it whatever you do with it, are part of that vanguard. Please Kinect responsibly.

--Jonathan Hall

Index

Made in the USA
Lexington, KY
17 October 2012